Sustaining Trade Reform

DIRECTIONS IN DEVELOPMENT
Trade

Sustaining Trade Reform

Institutional Lessons from Argentina and Peru

Elías A. Baracat, J. Michael Finger,
Raúl León Thorne, and Julio J. Nogués

THE WORLD BANK
Washington, D.C.

1 2 3 4 16 15 14 13

ISBN (paper): 978-0-8213-9986-6
ISBN (electronic): 978-0-8213-9987-3
DOI: 10.1596/978-0-8213-9986-6

Cover photo: © APM Terminals Callao—Terminal Norte Multipropósito del Puerto del Callao. Used with permission; further permission required for reuse.
Cover design: Naylor Design.

Library of Congress Cataloging-in-Publication Data

Baracat, Elías.
Sustaining trade reform : institutional lessons from Argentina and Peru / by Elías A. Baracat, J. Michael Finger, Raúl León Thorne, and Julio J. Nogués.
pages cm—(Directions in development)
Includes bibliographical references.
ISBN 978-0-8213-9986-6 (alk. paper) — ISBN 978-0-8213-9987-3 (ebk.)
1. Argentina—Commercial policy. 2. Argentina—Commerce. 3. Peru—Commercial policy. 4. Peru—Commerce. I. World Bank. II. Title.
HF1480.5.B366 2013
382'.30982—dc23 2013022141

Contents

Boxes

Figures

Tables

Acknowledgments

Francis Ng, of the World Bank's International Trade and Integration Team, has provided substantive and administrative support throughout the preparation of this book. He guided preparation of the proposal and provided critical data and other information as the work was conducted. He also managed the preparation of a final manuscript and has been an efficient interface between the authors and the publications process. The authors wish to express their appreciation for the support he has provided. Likewise, we wish to express our appreciation for the support provided by Aaditya Mattoo, manager of the International Trade and Integration Team of the World Bank.

The authors wish also to thank a number of persons for providing extensive information and insightful comments. The analysis of Peru's reforms owes much to the willingness of Javier Illescas, Eduardo Ferreyros, Jaime Thorne, Mercedes Aráoz, Fernando Zavala, Marisol Guiulfo, Julio Velarde, Renzo Rossini, and Luis Alberto León to share their experiences with the authors. Likewise, we acknowledge with gratitude the comments of Zafer Mustafaoglu on the Argentina chapter and of Carlos Silva-Jauregui on the Peru chapter.

The support provided in Lima by Judith Vergara is also gratefully acknowledged, as is the skillful and caring copyediting provided by Linda Stringer of Publications Professionals LLC. Aziz Gokdemir, World Bank Publications, was the production manager. His input is also gratefully acknowledged.

Financial support from the World Bank's Research Support Budget is also gratefully acknowledged.

About the Authors

Elías A. Baracat was the founding president of the Argentine International Trade Commission. He is currently a prominent consultant on Argentine commercial policy and the administration of that policy. *E-mail:* eliasbaracat@hotmail.com.

J. Michael Finger organized the first trade policy research unit at the World Bank. He has also served as visiting professor at universities in Australia, China, Sweden, and Texas. *E-mail:* michael.finger@comcast.net.

Raúl León Thorne was a founding member of the Commission on Antidumping and Safeguards in Peru. He has also served as a member on several important World Trade Organization dispute panels. *E-mail:* rleont@speedy.com.pe.

Julio J. Nogués is a member of the National Academy of Economy in Argentina. He has also served as trade representative of Argentina to the United States and undersecretary in Argentina's Ministry of Economics. *E-mail:* jnogues@fibertel.com.ar.

Abbreviations

AFIP	Administración Federal de Ingresos Públicos, or Federal Public Revenue Administration (Argentina)
APEC	Asia-Pacific Economic Cooperation
APRA	Alianza Popular Revolucionaria Americana, or American Popular Revolutionary Alliance (Peru)
ATPA	Andean Trade Preference Act
ATPEA	Andean Trade Preference Expansion Act
AVE	ad valorem tax equivalent
BCRP	Banco Central de Reserva del Perú, or Central Reserve Bank of Peru
CAN	Comunidad Andina de Naciones, or Andean Community of Nations
CNCE	Comisión Nacional de Comercio Exterior, or National Commission on Foreign Trade (Argentina)
DL	Decretos Legislativos, or Legislative Decree (Peru)
DS	Decreto Supremo, or Supreme Decree (Peru)
EFTA	European Free Trade Area
EU	European Union
FOB	free-on-board (price)
FTA	free trade agreement
FTAA	Free Trade Area of the Americas
GATT	General Agreement on Tariffs and Trade
GDP	gross domestic product
IMF	International Monetary Fund
INDEC	Instituto Nacional de Estadística y Censos, or National Institute of Statistics and Censuses
INDECOPI	Instituto Nacional de Defensa de la Competencia y de la Protección de la Propiedad Intelectual, or National Institute for the Defense of Competition and the Protection of Intellectual Property (Peru)

MEF	Ministerio de Economía y Finanzas, or Ministry of Economy and Finance (Peru)
MERCOSUR	Mercado Común del Sur, or the Common Market of the South
MINCETUR	Ministerio de Comercio Exterior y Turismo, or Ministry of Foreign Commerce and Tourism (Peru)
MMM	Marco Macroeconómico Multianual, or Multiannual Macroeconomic Framework (Peru)
NAFTA	North American Free Trade Agreement
NAL	nonautomatic license
ONCCA	Oficina Nacional de Control Comercial Agropecuario, or National Office of Agricultural Trade Control (Argentina)
QR	quantitative restriction
RM	Resolución Ministerial, or Ministerial Resolution (Peru)
SENASA	Servicio Nacional de Sanidad Agraria, or National Service of Agricultural Sanitation (Peru)
WTO	World Trade Organization
YPF	Yacimientos Petrolíferos Fiscales (Argentine energy company)

Systems determine outcomes. Public policy will only get the economics it needs, or indeed that society needs, if the processes, the institutions, and the individuals responsible for developing it are receptive to good economics, and responsive to it.

—Gary Banks, Chairman, Australian Productivity Commission
Opening address to the 40th Australian Conference of Economists
Symposium, Canberra, July 14, 2011

CHAPTER 1

Introduction

Background

Trade reform in Latin America in the 1980s and 1990s was in significant part a reform of policy-making institutions. The institutions that existed when the reforms began had been created in response to particular protectionist pressures at particular times, and afterward they were controlled by the interests on whose behalf they had been created.[1] Reform consequently involved the disbanding of such institutions and the creation of new ones.

The institutional changes reflected two overlapping objectives: (a) to overcome the advantage that protection seekers enjoyed in then-existing procedures and (b) to change the culture of policy making from one based on long-standing relationships to one based on unified, objective, and transparent assessment of economic costs and benefits. Procedures for managing industry requests or pressures for protection were structured around the same economywide principles that provided the political and philosophical basis for liberalization programs. Accommodating trade policies and trade policy processes to the demands of the General Agreement on Tariffs and Trade (GATT), which later became the World Trade Organization (WTO), was an important part of this transformation.[2]

This book was prompted by preliminary evidence suggesting that the reforms have been better sustained in Peru than in Argentina. Peru has continued its liberalization whereas Argentina has imposed a number of new trade restrictions. Moreover, decisions on many of Argentina's restrictions have not gone through the new mechanisms.

The objective of this book is to draw lessons from Peruvian and Argentine experience that will be useful to governments that want to maintain an open trade regime. From a positive perspective, we want to identify what the Peruvian government has done that has kept its liberalization moving forward. The Peru study focuses on how reform leaders in that country have reinforced the evolution of a new management culture and how they have disseminated widely in Peruvian society a positive vision of Peru in the international economy.

The Argentine study documents how the country has reverted to a highly protectionist trade policy and to its old management culture. A key aspect of this experience is how, within the WTO system, the government of Argentina has been able to reverse many of the reforms that entry into that system had supported. The principal lesson we draw from the Argentine experience is that maintaining a liberal trade policy is a matter of continuing *domestic* commitment to such policy. We conclude that WTO support for the governments of developing countries, as well as those of other countries that want to maintain open trade policies, depends on how such countries' legal structures and politics pay attention to and support the domestic politics of reform—not on the legal demands that membership imposes.

Analytical Framework

The analytical framework for the book draws substantially from the institutional economics literature. As does mainstream economics, institutional economics presumes rational choice by actors, but institutional economics then pays particular attention to how this choice is bounded by the actors' conceptions of the relevant "science" (how objective things relate to and affect one another), by the amount and the nature of the information available to the actors, by the values against which actors judge both processes and outcomes, and by the structures provided by the legal environment in which decision makers operate.[3]

Institutional economics brings attention to the processes through which things are done. In this book, we apply it to the processes through which trade policy decisions are made. Implicitly or explicitly, these processes impose criteria on decisions that may neither capture the interests of all interested parties nor approximate what economics would bring forward as the costs versus the benefits of the proposed action. Decisions to restrict imports are often not made by agents acting for all of the interested parties—that is, import users, exporters, and competing domestic producers—but through processes that producer interests have often dominated. Trade policy reform has often taken the form of changes of processes that brought other interests into play.

Levels of Societal Structure

Institutional economics examines several levels of societal structure. The following breakdown of four levels of social analysis is based on a schema elaborated by Oliver E. Williamson (2000, 597), an institutional economist who has won an economics Nobel Prize:

- *Level 1: Embodied values, customs, traditions, and norms*. Sociology has perhaps paid more attention to this level of social structure than has economics. As Knight (1992, 15) states, "Here social institutions are best understood as those rules that establish and maintain the typologies of similarity and the logic of appropriateness." As we will explain in chapters 2 and 3, differences between Argentina and Peru begin at this level: in different conceptions of the relationship between the country and the rest of the world and in different conceptions of the value of formalized processes in making and applying economic policy.

Another difference that we will develop is one suggested by the quote from Gary Banks (2011) with which we began this book: Are trade policy decisions framed within a context in which economic concepts provide the standard for what is an appropriate outcome? Or are these decisions framed and evaluated in a different context? For example, in matters of international trade, there is always a sense of "ours" versus "theirs." When President Cristina Fernández de Kirchner states that Argentina should import "not one nail" (as we will discuss in chapters 3 and 4), she appeals perhaps to a sense of patriotism rather than of economics.

- *Level 2: Structured rules and procedures that sometimes have explicit expression in law but that are often shaped more by tradition.* Shifts of the rules and procedures that shape national decisions on trade policy—as well as the ways evolution of the GATT/WTO system has influenced these shifts—are important parts of the trade policy story. Mancur Olson (1971, 1982) pays particular attention to the "stickiness" of institutions and how they keep in play only a particular group of interests and values even after the changed environment requires consideration of additional or different groups in order to reach socially optimal outcomes. He also calls attention to social shocks, such as the economic turmoil experienced by Argentina and Peru in the 1980s, as providing opportunity for change.

- *Level 3: Application of rules and standards or how the rules and procedures are administered in practice.* For example, this level considers how decisions on import restrictions are made, through trade remedy or other mechanisms. Although in economic logic imposing and removing trade restrictions are opposite directions on the same scale, they are done in the GATT/WTO system through separate procedures. Within the system, new restrictions are created through trade remedy processes, and they provide a relatively clear demarcation between level 2 (making the rules) and level 3 (applying them). Reductions of restrictions during the GATT/WTO era are sometimes made through unilateral national decisions and sometimes through reciprocal negotiations. Here, the distinction between levels 2 and 3 is less clear. Negotiation procedures are often less structured and more responsive to opportunity.

  Another complication is the existence of both GATT/WTO rules and national rules. Both levels have rules about the circumstances in which a trade restriction may be imposed (for example, when imports "injure" domestic producers) and rules about the procedures that must be followed to determine whether these circumstances exist.

- *Level 4: Resource allocation.* This level addresses the economics of how a policy, such as a tariff, affects resource allocation and the efficiency with which the economy uses resources.

As this schema indicates, institutional economics covers a wide range of social structure and human behavior. Without insisting that the topics taken up in this book might not be described as "mainstream economics," we distinguish our analysis by our attention to process and by our attention to attempts by policy makers to use changes of level 2 and 3 rules and procedures to change the level 1 concepts and standards by which their societies evaluate trade policy. Box 1.1 provides a profile of the many dimensions of social structure and human

---

Box 1.1 What *Institution* Means in *Institutional Economics*

Practitioners of institutional economics have analyzed a broad spectrum of social structure and human behavior. The following quotations were selected to provide an appreciation of the range of dimensions of social structure and behavior that different scholars who are recognized as institutional economists have taken up.

Walton H. Hamilton (1963, 84):

> Institution is the verbal symbol which for want of a better describes a cluster of social usages. It connotes a way of thought or action of some prevalence and permanence, which is embedded in the habits of a group or the customs of a people. In ordinary speech it is another word for procedure, convention, or arrangement; in the language of books it is the singular of which the mores or the folkways are the plural. Institutions fix the confines of and impose form upon the activities of human beings.

Douglass C. North (1990, 97):

> Institutions are the humanly devised constraints that structure political, economic, and social interaction. They consist of both informal constraints (sanctions, taboos, customs, traditions, and codes of conduct) and formal rules (constitutions, laws, property rights).

Malcolm Rutherford (2001, 174):

> For Veblen, as for other institutionalists, institutions were more than merely constraints on individual action, but embodied generally accepted ways of thinking and behaving. Thus, institutions worked to mold the preferences and values of individuals brought up under their sway.

Jonathan Turner (1997, 6):

> [Institutions are] a complex of positions, roles, norms, and values lodged in particular types of social structures and organizing relatively stable patterns of human activity with respect to fundamental problems in producing life-sustaining resources, in reproducing individuals, and in sustaining viable societal structures within a given environment.

Richard R. Nelson and Bhaven N. Sampat (2001):

> Some authors identify institutions with the rules of the game, or with the governing structures controlling the players, others with the way the game is played, others with systems of beliefs and expectations. (37)

box continues next page

Box 1.1 What *Institution* Means in *Institutional Economics* *(continued)*

> North (1990) takes pains to state that … institutions define the environment within which organizations can grow up and within which they operate, but that organizations are not institutions. (37)
>
> For Williamson, standard organizational forms are among the most important of an economy's institutions. (38)
>
> Institutions influence, or define, the ways in which economic actors get things done, in contexts involving human interaction. (39)
>
> Our suggestion is to associate the term "institutions" with "social technologies" that have been regarded by the relevant social group as standard in the context. (40)

Geoffrey M. Hodgson (1998, 168):

> The core ideas of institutionalism concern institutions, habits, rules, and their evolution. However, intuitionalists do not attempt to build a single, general model on the basis of these ideas. Instead, these ideas facilitate a strong impetus toward specific and historically located approaches to analysis.

behavior that institutional economists have brought out. In the following section, we identify the particular insights of institutional economics on which we will build.

Insights of Institutional Economics

The first insight of institutional economics on which we will build is a focus on process.[4] Reaching different policies is often a matter of changing the process through which they are made. Reform of analytical process through the Australian Productivity Commission and its antecedents has been an important part of policy reform in Australia.[5] In our previous study (*Safeguards and Antidumping in Latin American Trade Liberalization: Fighting Fire with Fire*), we found that Latin American reform leaders paid attention to changing the processes for managing domestic pressures for protection (Finger and Nogués 2006). They saw changing the processes as an important part of introducing reforms—and also of sustaining them.

The second insight is an attention to feedback effects. In the prologue to their classic study of how the Reciprocal Trade Agreement Act had changed U.S. trade policy, Bauer, Pool, and Dexter (1972, ix) remind that "individual and group interests get grossly redefined by the operation of the social institutions through which they must work." Or in Walton Hamilton's (1963, 89) nimble phrasing, "Institutions and human actions, complements and antitheses, are forever remaking each other in the endless drama of the social process."

Combining these insights—focus on process and attention to feedback—Hodgson (1998, 185) comments that in institutional economics, the chicken-or-egg question is not "Which came first?" but "What process explains the evolution of both?"

Another implication of the bounded rationality that influences the evolution of economic institutions is that those that emerge will not necessarily support economic efficiency. In work that earned him a Nobel Prize, Douglass C. North separates successful examples of economic development from unsuccessful examples according to how the institutions for ownership, use, and exchange of economic resources have developed.[6] The "flaws" (relative to the standards of economic theory) in institutional structures have been found to vary from environment to environment; hence, institutional economics tends to be more an application of key concepts to concrete situations than an all-embracing theory.[7]

The following insights from institutional economics on which we build are interrelated:

- Institutional economics deals with governance failure as well as with market failure.
- Good economics is neither guaranteed by nor inconsistent with democracy.

One of the key elements in trade policy is a collective action problem. Individual producers, because there are fewer of them, have more at stake in a decision to impose or not impose an import restriction than do individual consumers. In addition, producers are usually more aware of how their interests will be affected. For more than a century, the U.S. Congress set tariff rates by direct vote. Elmer Schattschneider (1935) identified the "logrolling" process that evolved and explained how producer interests dominated the process. The United States was a high-tariff country during this period.

The U.S. Reciprocal Trade Agreements Act of 1934 initiated a new process: reciprocal negotiation of rates with other countries. This process shifted the domestic politics of tariffs to a congressional act that delegated to the president the authority to declare the rates he had negotiated to be in legal effect. Exporters had a direct interest in the passage of that act and became an important force in making U.S. trade policy. The change of procedure changed the leverage of interests that bore on trade policy, which in turn changed the dynamic of how trade policy evolved.

Relative to "good economics"—a process that would accurately weigh the impact of a policy on all affected parties—the initial process was biased in that it overemphasized import-competing interests, and the second because it overemphasized export interests. Export mercantilism—by leading to a reduction of trade restrictions—did, however, produce a better economic result than import mercantilism had produced.[8]

In their recent book, *Why Nations Fail: The Origins of Power, Prosperity, and Poverty*, Daron Acemoglu and James Robinson (2012, 43) argue "that while economic institutions are critical for determining whether a country is poor or prosperous, it is politics and political institutions that determine what economic institutions a country has." They provide a number of historical examples to demonstrate that societies with "inclusive" institutional structures have generally enjoyed continuing economic growth, whereas those with "extractive" structures have not. An inclusive political system, they argue, will support the evolution of good economic institutions and over the long term will engender economic growth. In contrast, if a political system is dominated by a narrow elite, that elite will often apply the power of the state exclusively to advance its own interests. The elite will "extract" from the economy for its exclusive benefit and, in doing so, will stifle individual initiative. Economic growth will lag.

The reader should keep in mind that in Acemoglu and Robinson's analytical structure, *inclusive* is defined by its political nature, whereas *extractive* is defined as an economic result. It does not imply that inclusive—as politics—guarantees good economics or that extractive trade and other economic policies come only from autocratic (noninclusive) political systems.[9] The ways that tariffs were set in the United States before the Reciprocal Trade Agreements Act—by direct vote of Congress—could hardly be described as undemocratic. Also, chapter 3 will point out that the restrictive trade policies recently introduced by the Argentine government have been widely popular. Candidates who criticized them did poorly in recent elections. In the United States, as in Argentina, elections were free and the franchise widely enjoyed. Thus, under democracy the United States went from growth-inhibiting trade policies to open, growth-supportive trade policies. Argentina, likewise under democracy, went from open trade policies to highly restrictive policies. And in the past decade, Argentina has moved back from reforms introduced in the 1990s that had made the process of trade policy governance more inclusive of interested party participation. Chile and Peru began their moves toward open trade policies—and toward trade policy governance institutions more inclusive of interested party participation—under autocratic governments; subsequent democratic governments in both countries continued the reforms.[10]

The Political Economy of Trade Policy

The book will also draw from a literature that might be labeled "the political economy of trade policy." As they begin their review of this literature, Bagwell and Staiger (2010, 224) put forward one of its key premises:

> Most trade-policy decisions that governments face today arise in the context of a variety of international commitments that must be considered; hence, the study of commercial policy in international trade has in effect become the study of trade agreements, in which the GATT/WTO plays a central role.

Regarding the liberalization experiences we have studied, this statement is both descriptively incorrect and analytically misleading. It suggests that countries determine their policies through bargaining with other countries—that the multilateral negotiations are the process from which "home" and "foreign" policies emerge simultaneously.[11]

With Mexico's bargaining of the North American Free Trade Agreement with Canada and the United States being the exception, Latin American trade policy reform has been in large part unilateral. Tariff reductions were not made through the process of GATT bargaining; indeed, the bound rates these countries attached to the Uruguay Round agreements were ceiling bindings, two or three times higher than the rates already being applied. (Mexico, too, has WTO-bound rates averaging about 35 percent, about three times the average for the applied most-favored-nation rates.)

Likewise for GATT/WTO rules on antidumping and other "trade remedies," Latin American governments were not bargaining with other countries over the content of these rules; they were using the rules—as they existed—to restructure domestic policy-making institutions in such a way as to remove a burdensome accumulation of institutions and regulations and to ensure that the philosophies and interests that supported the ongoing reforms would have a voice in the management of pressures for protection that might arise in the future.

This approach, some might remark, amounts to a "commitments model," but that label is also analytically misleading and is at best crudely descriptive. A key finding of *Fighting Fire with Fire* (Finger and Nogués 2006) was that GATT/WTO rules (their procedural dimensions more than their economic dimensions) provided a means through which reformers hoped to change the *culture* of policy making from one based on relationships to one based on unified, objective, and transparent processes. The focus was on changing what would have value in domestic politics rather than forcing domestic politics to accept something forced on it by an international agreement. Reform leaders used GATT/WTO rules in their struggles within domestic politics; however, they used them more as a template for managing domestic policy issues than as an international commitment they could place in front of any domestic interest pressing for protection.[12]

A part of the political economy of trade policy that our findings support is the *bicycle theory*—the idea that unless the positive side of trade reform is made visible through international negotiations, liberalization's momentum will languish and protectionist pressures will ascend. Consistent with this proposition, interests in Peru favoring liberal (open) trade policies have maintained the political dynamics of the reform effort by negotiating a series of bilateral trade agreements. Although the bicycle theory is more often cited with regard to multilateral negotiations, Peru's use of bilateral negotiations with the United States is an extension of the bicycle theory to regional negotiations.

Policy Makers' Choices and Economic Analysis

Institutional economics has paid considerable attention to understanding how decisions are made. Here we will elaborate aspects of this analysis that bear particularly on the content of this book. Our takeoff point is the following quotation from Douglass North (1990, 17):

> The motivation of the actors is more complicated (and their preferences less stable) than assumed in received theory. More controversial (and less understood) among the behavioral assumptions, usually, is the implicit one that the actors possess cognitive systems that provide *true* models of the worlds about which they make

> choices or, at the very least, that the actors receive information that leads to convergence of divergent initial models. This is patently wrong. (emphasis in original)

North (1990, 40) goes on to identify the various influences that will affect a policy maker's decisions. Among them are ideas, ideologies, convictions, and interests.

To understand a policy decision so that one can develop ideas about how the decision might be changed, analysts should consider the possibility of differences between the way they see the problem that the policy should resolve and the way a decision maker might see it:

- *Different interests*. This difference refers to the interest groups that receive weight in the economics part of the decision maker's preference function. It also relates to the noneconomic impacts of the policy in question. The familiar phrase "Trade policy is foreign policy" is an example. "To a trade economist, trade policy is always a non sequitur" is another way of stating that the reasons behind trade policy are not often those taught in economics class. Article XX of GATT provides other examples in that it allows measures necessary to protect public morals; to protect human, animal, or plant life or health; and so forth, even though such measures might be trade restrictive. It asks, however, that such restrictions not arbitrarily or unjustifiably discriminate among countries or be "disguised restrictions" on international trade. The general sense of the article is that among the policies available to achieve the objective, the country chose the least trade restrictive one.

- *Different economics*. The policy maker may be thinking within a *partial equilibrium model*, aware of the immediate impact of a trade restriction on the protected interests but unaware of the impact on user costs or on long-run productivity.

- *Different frame of reference*. This difference is about level 1, where we deal with values and norms; in the language cited previously, it refers to "topologies of similarities and the logic of appropriateness." Should, say, democratic values be the basis for the policy choice? If so, operationally the standard of appropriateness might be to choose the policies most consistent with the will of the people, as expressed through existing political processes. Or should economic values be the basis for the decision? Using that basis would mean that the standard would be to choose the policy that best advances economic welfare or to choose a process within which the economic impacts on all interested parties have equal weight.

We might label the first of these processes *politics as usual*, but in doing so we do not want to be pejorative. As chapter 3 will show, Argentina's recent trade policies are not those that grade out high as economics, but they have been put in place by a democratically elected government and have been endorsed in recent elections. The *economics* is shaped by the considerations that go into the process by which the decision is made. Later in the book we will describe this as *backfill economics*.

Moreover, choosing a policy that is bad economics need not imply a venal policy maker. It might imply an instinct to apply a different topology of similarity and logic of appropriateness.[13] David Henderson (1986) points out the frequent application by policy makers of "do-it-yourself economics," which are unrelated to the characteristic ways of thinking of professional economists.[14]

Furthermore, in the decision process, determining which facts are relevant can be related to the standard against which the outcome is evaluated. On this, Thorstein Veblen (1915, 11) postulates:

> Those features of the facts at hand are salient and substantial upon which the dominant interest of the time throws its light. Any given ground of distinction will seem insubstantial to any one who habitually apprehends the facts in question from a different point of view and values them for a different purpose.

On policy matters, there is considerable risk that policy makers and economists will talk past each other, that they will present arguments made within different topologies of similarities and logics of appropriateness. Cognitive science would see this circumstance as a matter of economists and policy makers conceptualizing within different *frames*. To people conceptualizing within different frames, the same information can have a very different meaning and relevance.

As for our own position, our objective is to find policy processes that respect both economic and democratic values: decision processes that accurately weigh the impact of a policy on all affected parties.

Management of Pressures for Protection: Formal versus Informal Procedures

In our analysis, we apply a distinction between *formal* and *informal* procedures for deciding to apply trade restrictions. We do so because rules and transparent process have been the basis in many countries for overcoming the governance failure from the oft-mentioned tendency for concentrated producer interests to dominate more diffused user and consumer interests. Theodore Lowi (1964) was among the first to demonstrate how shifting decision making away from "general politics" into such a structure would change the policy outcome.

We pay particular attention to the adoption of GATT/WTO trade remedy procedures. The installation of such procedures has been a major part of Latin American reformers' attempt both to remove the accumulation of restrictions in place and to create a culture of management of pressures for protection that would support an overall process of liberalization.

The GATT/WTO template for trade remedies[15] provides for the recognition of and participation by interested parties, for open procedures according to previously announced criteria, and for publication of the decisions and the reasons for decisions—in fact and in law. It also prescribes time limits and periodic review of the usefulness of keeping a restriction in place. In short, these rules provide for accountable, contestable processes that are based on criteria with operational meaning, in which all stakeholders have an opportunity to participate.[16]

Viewing GATT/WTO trade remedies from the perspective of the global system, Finger (2012, 418) concludes that they have been a useful part of the liberal trading system:

> They have provided process and flexibility for WTO member governments to manage internal pressures for protection within a generally liberal trade policy. They have helped to keep the application of new restrictions under sufficient discipline that their use has minimally compromised the momentum of liberalization the reciprocal negotiations have created, and they have managed the application of new restrictions in such a way that unsuccessful protection seekers have not organized to overturn the system—they have brought protection-seekers to accept 'No' for an answer.

We view the accommodation of Argentine and Peruvian procedures with GATT/WTO stipulations within the deeper context of institutional change. We do so to carry analysis of how international cooperation has or has not supported reform beyond a simple interpretation of commitment as national submission to international rules. The general thesis here is that international cooperation has been useful when it has recognized and influenced domestic sovereignty over economic regulation, but it has not been useful when approached as a matter of international regulation of national actions.

Content of the Following Chapters

Chapters 2 and 3 analyze the management of trade policy in Peru and Argentina, respectively, roughly from 2001 to 2010. These studies cover more or less what has happened since the reforms that were studied in *Fighting Fire with Fire* (Finger and Nogués 2006). As our work progressed, the Argentina study paid particular attention to the application of restrictions outside the procedural and governance reforms of the 1990s. In Peru, the focus of the study turned toward the strategy that the government had used to maintain support for the reforms, the negotiation of free trade agreements with major economic powers being a critical part of that strategy.

Chapter 4 brings forward key findings of the country studies and provides a comparison of the two cases. Chapter 5 takes up the usefulness of institutional economics as an analytical framework for the study of trade reform experiences. It also offers suggestions for research that could help the international community continue to support such reform.

Notes

1. This was one of the key findings of the study by Finger and Nogués (2006) of Latin American trade liberalization in the 1980s and 1990s. We were not, however, the first to observe this pattern. In his pathbreaking study of trade policy in developing

countries, Bela Balassa (1971, xv) observed, "The existing system of protection in many developing countries can be described as the historical result of actions taken at different times and for different reasons. These actions have been in response to the particular circumstances of the situation, and have often been conditioned by the demands of special interest groups."

2. This is not to say that reform leaders saw the role of international organizations solely as a template for changing domestic policy management structures. They also saw international organizations—and here perhaps more the World Bank and the International Monetary Fund (IMF) than the GATT/WTO—as endorsements that would have influence in domestic politics, particularly because the World Bank and the IMF augmented their endorsements with money. It still follows, however, that for the reforms to stick after these endorsements ended, they would have to be—in ways taken up in this book—institutionalized.
3. Compare this statement of Douglass North (1990, 111): "There is nothing the matter with the rational actor paradigm that could not be cured by a healthy awareness of the complexity of human motivation and the problems that arise from information processing."
4. John R. Commons, one of the first practitioners of institutional economics in the United States, emphasized this point; Rutherford (2001) provides an introduction to the work of earlier institutional economists.
5. The Australian Productivity Commission (2003) provides a history of the introduction of the economywide perspective into Australian policy making.
6. North (1990, 1991) elaborates this point.
7. Hodgson (1998, 2003) elaborates this point.
8. Finger (2012) posits that the trade remedy process in the United States is evolving toward one in which importer interests have significant weight.
9. *Democratic* and *autocratic* as politics do not map one to one into *inclusive* and *extractive* as economics.
10. The Economist Intelligence Unit's Democracy Index ranks 167 countries: from Norway, at the top with an index value of 9.8, to Democratic People's Republic of Korea, with an index value of 1.1. The United States ranks 19th; the subject countries here, Argentina and Peru, rank 51st and 56th, respectively. However, the index values for Argentina and Peru differ from the value for the United States by less than the United States lags Norway.
11. With regard to level 1 social structure, the statement is perhaps more an expression of what Bagwell and Staiger (2010) acknowledge as expressions of their cultural values than a description of the content of the study of commercial policy.
12. Indeed, WTO rules on the use of trade remedies provided less of a legal barrier against new protection than some of the reform leaders had hoped. Protection seekers, armed with briefs from Washington and Brussels experts, presented a solid argument that they were being denied protection that U.S. and European Union experience showed was acceptable under WTO rules.
13. North (1990, 40) refers to empirical work that suggests trade-offs among the various elements; that is, the lower the price of one—of ideas, ideologies, convictions, or interests in relation to another—the more that one will weigh in decisions.
14. Henderson (1986, 10) also describes this phenomenon as "economic policy without economics."

15. We refer to the agreements on safeguards, on subsidies, and on countervailing measures and on the implementation of article VI of GATT 1994 (the antidumping agreement).
16. Thus, as one can distinguish analytically between the formal and informal sectors of the economy, one can distinguish between the formal and informal sectors of government.

References

Acemoglu, Daron, and James Robinson. 2012. *Why Nations Fail: The Origins of Power, Prosperity, and Poverty*. New York: Crown.

Australian Productivity Commission. 2003. *From Industry Assistance to Productivity: 30 Years of 'the Commission.'* Canberra: Australian Productivity Commission.

Bagwell, Kyle, and Robert W. Staiger. 2010. "The World Trade Organization: Theory and Practice." *Annual Reviews of Economics* 2 (1): 223–56.

Balassa, Bela. 1971. *The Structure of Protection in Developing Countries*. Baltimore, MD: Johns Hopkins University Press.

Banks, Gary. 2011. "Economics, Economists, and Public Policy in Australia." Opening address to the 40th Australian Conference of Economists Symposium, "Does Australian Public Policy Get the Economics It Deserves?" Canberra, July 14. http://www.pc.gov.au/__data/assets/pdf_file/0015/114234/20110714-economics.pdf.

Bauer, Raymond A., Ithiel de Sola Pool, and Lewis Anthony Dexter. 1972. *American Business and Public Policy: The Politics of Foreign Trade*. Chicago, IL: Aldine.

Finger, J. Michael. 2012. "Flexibilities, Rules, and Trade Remedies in the GATT/WTO System." In *The Oxford Handbook on the World Trade Organization*, edited by Amrita Narlikar, Martin Daunton, and Robert M. Stern, 418–40. Oxford, U.K.: Oxford University Press.

Finger, J. Michael, and Julio J. Nogués, eds. 2006. *Safeguards and Antidumping in Latin American Trade Liberalization: Fighting Fire with Fire*. New York: Palgrave Macmillan.

Hamilton, Walton H. 1963. "Institution." In *Encyclopaedia of the Social Sciences*, edited by Edwin R. A. Seligman and Alvin Johnson, vol. 8, 84–89. New York: Macmillan.

Henderson, David. 1986. *Innocence and Design: The Influence of Economic Ideas on Policy*. Oxford, U.K.: Blackwell.

Hodgson, Geoffrey M. 1998. "The Approach of Institutional Economics." *Journal of Economic Literature* 36 (1): 166–92.

———. 2003. "Introduction." In *Recent Developments in Institutional Economics*, edited by Geoffrey M. Hodgson, xi–xxix. Cheltenham, U.K.: Edward Elgar.

Knight, Jack. 1992. *Institutions and Social Conflict*. Cambridge, U.K.: Cambridge University Press.

Lowi, Theodore J. 1964. "American Business, Public Policy, Case-Studies, and Political Theory." *World Politics* 16 (4): 347–82.

Nelson, Richard R., and Bhaven N. Sampat. 2001. "Making Sense of Institutions as a Factor Shaping Economic Performance." *Journal of Economic Behavior and Organization* 44 (1): 31–54.

North, Douglass C. 1990. *Institutions, Institutional Change, and Economic Performance*. Cambridge, U.K.: Cambridge University Press.

———. 1991. "Institutions." *Journal of Economic Perspectives* 5 (1): 97–112.

Olson, Mancur. 1971. *The Logic of Collective Action*. Cambridge, MA: Harvard University Press.

———. 1982. *The Rise and Decline of Nations*. New Haven, CT: Yale University Press.

Rutherford, Malcolm. 2001. "Institutional Economics: Then and Now." *Journal of Economic Perspectives* 15 (3): 173–94.

Schattschneider, Elmer Eric. 1935. *Politics, Pressures, and the Tariff*. Englewood Cliffs, NJ: Prentice Hall. Reprint, Hamden, CT: Archon Books, 1963.

Turner, Jonathan. 1997. *The Institutional Order*. New York: Longman.

Veblen, Thorstein. 1915. *The Theory of the Leisure Class: An Economic Study of Institutions*. New York: Macmillan.

Williamson, Oliver E. 2000. "The New Institutional Economics: Taking Stock." *Journal of Economic Literature* 38 (3): 595–613.

CHAPTER 2

The Evolution of Trade Policy in Peru, 2001–11

Introduction

From 1990 to 2011, Peru experienced the most successful period of economic and social development in its history. Although it has not been recognized or publicized as such, we should consider Peru's success as a miracle when compared with the successes of Chile or Ireland. In two decades, Peru shifted from a vicious circle of decline to a virtuous circle of progress. Impressive macroeconomic breakthroughs came along with superlative achievements in social indicators.

According to statistics of Central Reserve Bank of Peru (Banco Central de Reserva del Perú, or BCRP), during those two decades gross domestic product (GDP) almost tripled, exports multiplied by 14, and international reserves multiplied by 37, while inflation was kept very low (averaging below 4 percent in the past decade). Public external debt has not increased (it stood at 13.7 percent at the end of 2011), and government income increased from 8.7 percent of GDP in 1989 to 19.2 percent in the first half of 2012.

At the same time, all social indicators showed similar progress. A recent study by Richard Webb,[1] Diether Beuermann, and Carla Revilla (2011) of the 200 poor rural districts finds that growth in rural capital income in the period from 2000 to 2010 was 6.6 percent per year compared with an average of 0.7 percent in the period from 1900 to 2000! Travel hours to the nearest city decreased from 14 in 2001 to 5 in 2011 owing to improvements in the national road network. In return, daily wages doubled and house values tripled, even as the indicators of infant mortality and extreme poverty fell by 50 percent during the period.

Focus of This Chapter

This chapter examines the continuation through the first decade of the 21st century of the trade policy reforms that began in Peru in the 1990s. The chapter focuses on governance and on the political and administrative decision-making processes through which Peruvian leaders have initiated and expanded these reforms.

In the 1990s, Peru began its shift toward integration into the global economy without a fully developed trade policy as such. Reform leaders began with concrete steps, such as reducing tariffs and revising foreign investment laws, through which leadership hoped to augment competitiveness in the local economy and to attract foreign investment. Through such reforms, leaders hoped to support the importation of the capital goods needed to improve domestic productivity and to expand Peru's export earnings. Some early but timid steps were taken toward improving access to foreign markets, but only in 2001 would negotiations with other countries become an active part of the emerging strategy.

The process of reform and the evolution of Peru's trade policy continue as we write this chapter. We focus here on the evolution of trade policy, but as we begin we remind the reader that trade policy is only part of a comprehensive reform. (A useful way to accentuate this fact is to point out that in the 1980s, when the World Bank was noted for its insistence on trade reform, its support for trade reform never accounted for as much as 10 percent of its lending or of its operational budget.)

We divide the process of reform into two stages: (a) during the successive authoritarian governments of Alberto Fujimori, between 1990 and 2000, and (b) under the succeeding democratic governments of Alejandro Toledo Manrique and Alan García Pérez, leader of the American Popular Revolutionary Alliance (Alianza Popular Revolucionaria Americana, or APRA).

This chapter starts with an analysis of the long-term vision of the policy makers of the Ministry of Economy and Finance and the Ministry of Foreign Commerce and Tourism for 2001–10 concerning the best path to guide the economic development of the country and to determine the extent to which economic openness has been a significant element in this growth scheme.

We move from there to an examination of some actions taken by the policy makers to implement this long-term vision and of some of the problems they faced. We will also examine how the authorities managed the main difficulties they had to deal with—both internally and externally—during the free trade agreement (FTA) negotiations with the United States and later with China. We will briefly review and compare the contents of the FTAs with China and the United States.

Finally, we will address success stories attributable to good practices of the National Institute for the Defense of Competition and the Protection of Intellectual Property (Instituto Nacional de Defensa de la Competencia y de la Protección de la Propiedad Intelectual, or INDECOPI) and the BCRP and will present a few final thoughts.

Economic Development: 1990–2000

We have already seen in *Safeguards and Antidumping in Latin American Trade Liberalization: Fighting Fire with Fire* (Finger and Nogués 2006, 249) that, in 1990,

> Fujimori became president in the context of one of the most severe economic and political crises of the country. The economy had experienced hyperinflation during the two preceding years while domestic production collapsed by 20 percent and public expenditure decreased even more because of the fall in revenue collection and the loss of the government's credit capacity. The presence of the government in the national territory was strongly reduced because of fiscal impoverishment, corruption, and growing terrorism led by Sendero Luminoso (Shining Path) and Túpac Amaru Revolutionary Movement. In general, quantity and quality of education, public health services, justice, police protection, and other government services declined severely.
>
> That collapse was attributed to APRA, the governing party since 1985. By 1990, terrorism had extended to most of Peru's territory and represented a real threat to the survival of democracy. This danger, along with the loss of popularity of interventionist, progovernment ideologies, opened the door to an extreme reaction in favor of liberal ideas.
>
> During the electoral campaign of 1990, candidate Vargas Llosa's liberal message was no longer regarded as a rationalization for big business and became, instead, a legitimate argument in favor of the national interest. Paradoxically, Fujimori was not elected on a liberal platform, but his lack of political ties or debts, his practical way of perceiving things, and the situation of emergency led him into the liberal path.

From the beginning, Fujimori implemented an aggressive structural reforms plan in order to liberalize the market.

Control Inflation

The first measures prioritized the fight against hyperinflation. In August 1990, a shock adjustment was made to the economy that was based on the rapid liberalization of controlled prices, the elimination of almost all subsidies, a scheduled reduction of monetary expansion, and an exchange rate dirty float. Inflation dropped substantially after 1991, as shown in figure 2.1.

Structural Changes

The structural changes made to the action framework of the Peruvian government in particular and to the economy at large were very deep.

First, the role of the government changed from mainly that of an interventionist through its public companies and pricing policies to that of a regulator of the free entrepreneurial activity of the private sector. An autonomous agency (now called Proinversión) was created to manage the privatization program. Regulation of the privatized economy was entrusted to autonomous agencies such as INDECOPI, the Supervisory Agency for Energy Investments and the Supervisory Agency for Private Investments in Telecommunications.

Important institutions such as the BCRP recovered their autonomy, capital flows and the use of foreign currency were liberalized, and a responsible and orderly fiscal management was established.

Figure 2.1 Average Annual Variation in Inflation Rate in Peru, 1990–2000

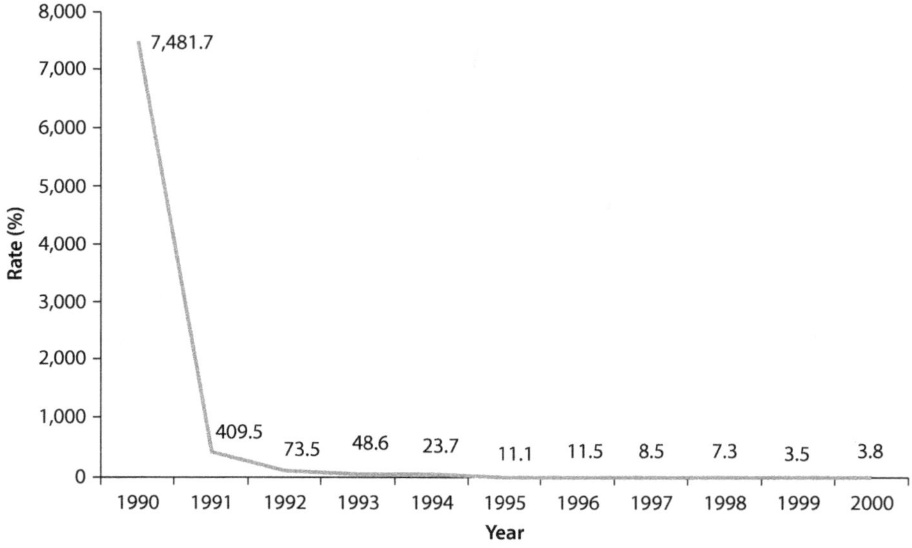

Source: Data from Central Reserve Bank of Peru.

The measures taken by Fujimori's administration broke the vicious circle that promoted inefficiency and corruption in which Peruvians had lived for several decades, and a virtuous circle emerged that allowed the private sector to do business. This situation brought about a significant flow of investments (a major portion of those investments resulted from the transfer of public companies to the private sector), which created many and better-paid jobs.

As a result of this new virtuous circle, the GDP recovered from its great fall of 1990 and behaved positively, mainly from 1993 to 1997 (figure 2.2). However, because of successive international crises and a wrongly restrictive fiscal policy, the GDP had a setback in 1998 and moderate growth for the rest of that decade.

During the 1990s, the current account had a negative balance, mainly because of a significant increase of capital goods imports that the private sector needed to carry out its investments. Those negative balances were funded by the significant inflow of private capital. A major part of that private capital came from the investments attracted by the in-depth privatization process of government companies that were transferred to the private sector. The foreign exchange reserves increased from US$1.304 billion in 1991 to US$8.180 billion in 2000 (table 2.1).

Historically, exports had been in the range of US$3 billion per year since the late 1970s. In the 1990s, they started an astounding growth pattern and went from US$3.28 billion in 1990 to US$6.955 billion in 2000 (table 2.2).

Figure 2.2 GDP Growth Rates, 1990–2000

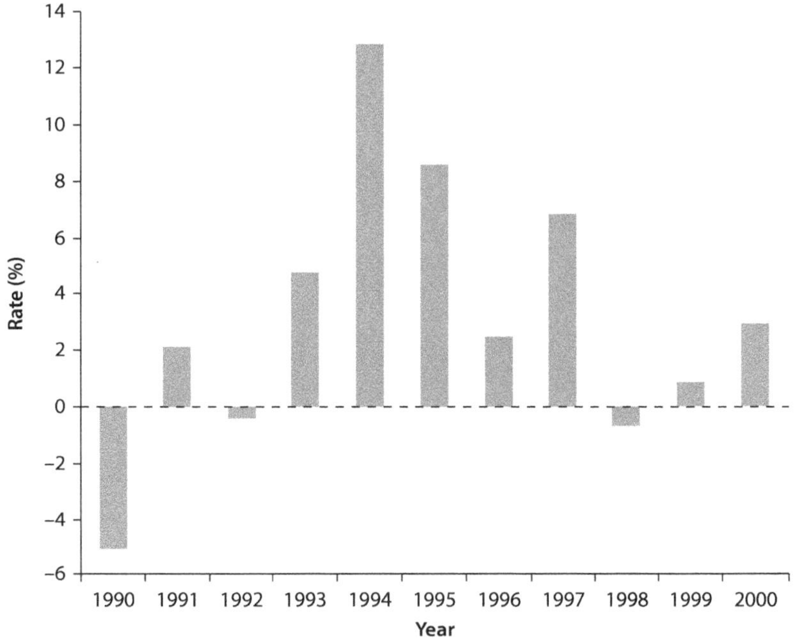

Source: Data from Central Reserve Bank of Peru.

Table 2.1 International Reserves, 1991–2000
US$ billions

	1991	*1992*	*1993*	*1994*	*1995*	*1996*	*1997*	*1998*	*1999*	*2000*
Net international reserves	1.304	2.001	2.742	5.718	6.641	8.540	10.169	9.183	8.404	8.180

Source: Data from Central Reserve Bank of Peru.

Although this growth rate is moderate compared with the big growth from 2000 to 2010, it is qualitatively very important because it meant moving beyond a stagnation stage that had lasted for decades.

Government revenue recovered from 8.7 percent of GDP in 1990 to 12.1 percent in 2000 (table 2.3).

The great deficits that the central government incurred in previous years were controlled, as shown in figure 2.3.

On November 19, 2000, a serious political crisis involving cases of gross corruption led to President Fujimori's resignation. A transitional government was immediately formed, led by Valentín Paniagua Corazao, the newly appointed interim president. After taking office on November 22, 2000, Paniagua concentrated on preparing a new presidential election process and on restoring democracy in the country. The first round of the election took place on April 8, and runoff voting took place June 3, 2001. Candidate Alejandro Toledo Manrique won the runoff vote.

Table 2.2 Balance of Payments, 1990–2000
US$ millions

	1990	1991	1992	1993	1994	1995	1996	1997	1998	1999	2000
I. Current account balance sheet	−1,459	−1,519	−1,916	−2,464	−2,701	−4,625	−3,644	−3,368	−3,336	−1,380	−1,546
1. Trade balance	358	−202	−423	−776	−1,075	−2,241	−1,987	−1,711	−2,462	−623	−403
a. Free-on-board exports	3,280	3,393	3,578	3,385	4,424	5,491	5,878	6,825	5,757	6,088	6,955
b. Free-on-board imports	−2,922	−3,595	−4,001	−4,160	−5,499	−7,733	−7,864	−8,536	−8,219	−6,710	−7,358
2. Services	−365	−413	−559	−550	−470	−733	−671	−786	−657	−588	−735
a. Exports	799	826	836	837	1,064	1,131	1,414	1,553	1,775	1,624	1,555
b. Imports	−1,164	−1,238	−1,396	−1,387	−1,534	−1,864	−2,085	−2,339	−2,432	−2,212	−2,290
3. Factor income	−1,733	−1,371	−1,392	−1,670	−1,944	−2,482	−1,899	−1,822	−1,204	−1,112	−1,410
a. Private	−35	−55	14	−287	−493	−1,080	−1,001	−1,324	−762	−549	−896
b. Public	−1,698	−1,316	−1,406	−1,383	−1,451	−1,402	−898	−498	−442	−563	−513
4. Current account transfers	281	467	458	532	788	832	912	952	987	943	1,001
II. Financial account	−713	−56	627	1,778	3,835	3,743	3,916	5,808	1,792	583	1,023
1. Private sector	47	139	4	1,300	3,958	3,072	4,338	2,833	1,805	1,678	1,481
2. Public sector	−1,067	−129	−411	341	−260	−172	−417	505	58	381	277
3. Short-term capital	308	−66	1,034	137	137	843	−5	2,471	−72	−1,476	−735
III. Exceptional financing	2,491	1,390	1,490	768	1,506	1,512	904	−711	244	24	−58
IV. Net errors and omissions	−301	972	515	575	338	295	756	4	295	−2	388
V. Central Reserve Bank of Peru net reserves flow (V = I + II + III + IV)	18	788	716	657	2,978	925	1,932	1,733	−1,005	−774	−192

Source: Data from Central Reserve Bank of Peru.
Note: Sums may not total because of rounding.

Table 2.3 Government Revenue as a Share of GDP, 1990–2000
Percent

	1990	*1991*	*1992*	*1993*	*1994*	*1995*	*1996*	*1997*	*1998*	*1999*	*2000*
GDP fiscal income	8.7	8.6	9.8	9.8	11.0	11.5	12.0	12.0	13.8	12.5	12.1

Source: Data from Central Reserve Bank of Peru.

Figure 2.3 Nonfinancial Public Sector Deficit as a Share of GDP, 1989–98

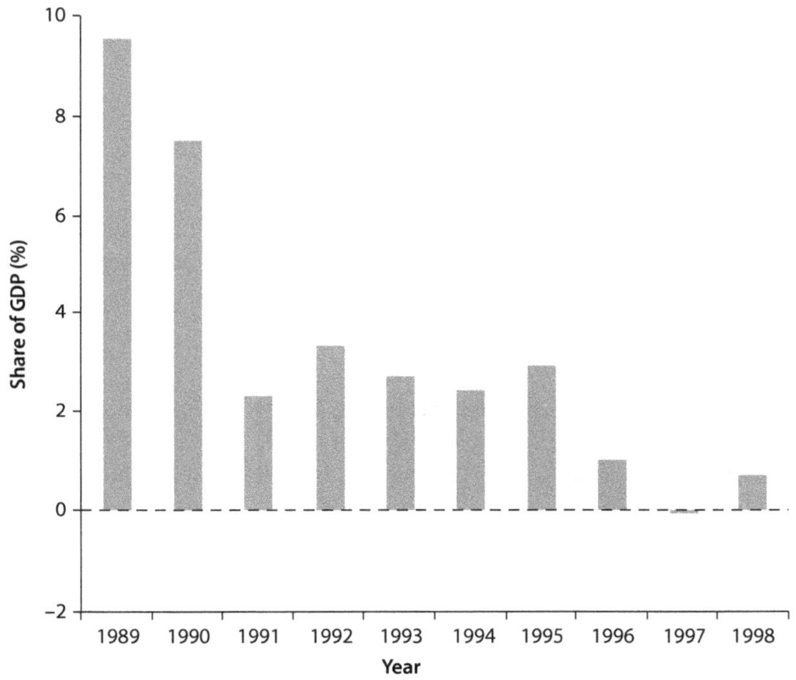

Source: Data from Central Reserve Bank of Peru.

Economic Development: 2001–10

The new president summoned prestigious and independent professionals for the essential positions in the economic administration. Among the most noted was Pedro Pablo Kuczynski, who was appointed minister of economy and finance.

Once the government was established, the president decided to continue the openness process initiated during the administration of Alberto Fujimori. Thus, the second stage of the current openness process started. As we will see, it has brought about impressive economic results.

In 2002, the economy began to grow significantly. Average yearly economic growth between 2000 and 2010 was more than 5 percent, and from 2005 to 2010, the average yearly growth rate was more than 7 percent (figure 2.4).

In real terms, GDP per capita increased 55 percent between 2001 and 2010, and 89 percent between 1990 and 2010, according to BCRP data (table 2.4).

Figure 2.4 GDP Growth Rates, 2000–10

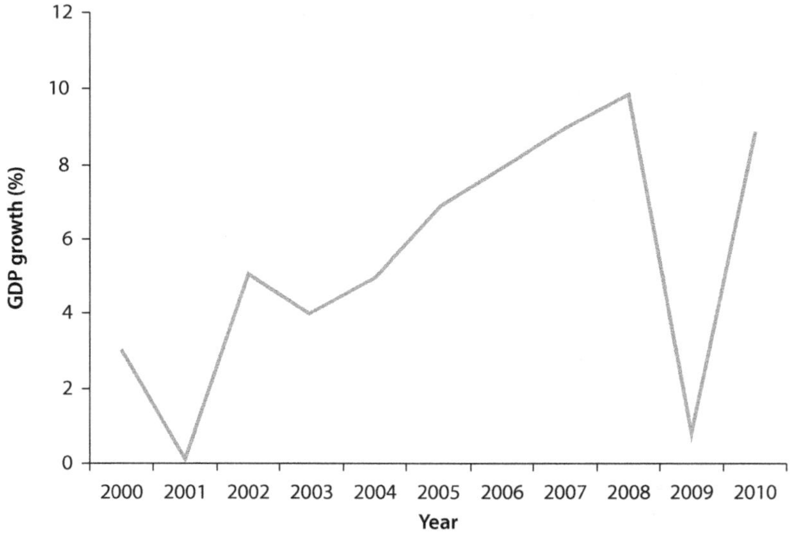

Source: Data from Central Reserve Bank of Peru.

At the same time, the exports of goods grew fivefold, from US$6.955 billion in 2000 to US$35.565 billion in 2010 (table 2.5) as a result of the significant investments in the private sector. The balance of trade has been positive since 2002.

In some years, the current account balance was negative mainly because of factor income, but the financial account of the private sector allowed a significant accumulation of resources so that the level of foreign exchange reserves has increased gradually in recent years (figure 2.5) and represents almost 40 times the amount of reserves that the country had at the beginning of the process. Similarly, in 2010, the private sector revenue in the financial account amounted to US$13,324 million compared with only US$47 million in 1990.

During the analysis period, 2000–10, inflation remained at appropriate levels (figure 2.6) and within the inflation rate goal range predicted by the BCRP.

The yearly inflation rate exceeded 5 percent only in 2008 (mainly because of the inflation of commodities), and it was significantly lower in all other years. Therefore, it remained within the goal range of the BCRP. Similarly, the exchange rate of nuevos soles per U.S. dollar has had a stable but downward trend (table 2.6) and followed a dirty float policy.

Developing a Long-Term Vision

The Political Constitution of Peru grants many powers to the president of Peru, who, as the head of the executive branch, appoints the 19 state ministers, presides over the Council of Ministers, and directly or indirectly appoints the officials in charge of the agencies that control the government and the entities that regulate the market.

Table 2.4 National Accounts, 1973–2010

Year	GDP (1)	Population (thousands) (2)	GDP per capita (S/. at 1994 prices) (3)	Percent variation (1)	Percent variation (2)	Percent variation (3)	Inflation	US$ millions: Exports of goods	US$ millions: Imports of goods	US$ millions: Trade balance
1973	73,980	14,348.1	5,156.1	6.5	2.8	3.5	13.8	1,111.8	1,033.0	78.8
1974	80,481	14,751.1	5,455.9	8.8	2.8	5.8	19.1	1,513.3	1,908.0	−394.7
1975	84,024	15,161.1	5,542.1	4.4	2.8	1.6	24	1,335.0	2,427.0	−1,092.0
1976	85,004	15,580.8	5,455.7	1.2	2.8	−1.6	44.6	1,344.0	2,016.0	−672.0
1977	85,529	16,010.8	5,342.0	0.6	2.8	−2.1	32.6	1,729.6	2,148.0	−418.4
1978	82,296	16,447.4	5,003.6	−3.8	2.7	−6.3	73.9	2,038.0	1,668.0	370.0
1979	83,920	16,886.5	4,969.7	2.0	2.7	−0.7	66.7	3,719.0	1,954.0	1,765.0
1980	90,354	17,324.2	5,215.5	7.7	2.6	4.9	60.1	3,950.6	3,089.5	861.1
1981	95,291	17,760.2	5,363.4	5.5	2.5	2.9	72.7	3,328.0	3,802.2	−474.2
1982	94,979	18,197.2	5,219.3	−0.3	2.5	−2.7	72.9	3,343.4	3,720.9	−377.5
1983	86,111	18,635.6	4,620.8	−9.3	2.4	−11.5	125.1	3,036.2	2,721.7	314.5
1984	89,382	19,075.9	4,685.6	3.8	2.4	1.4	111.5	3,193.4	2,166.5	1,026.9
1985	91,250	19,518.6	4,675.0	2.1	2.3	−0.2	158.3	3,021.4	1,822.6	1,198.8
1986	102,301	19,965.8	5,123.8	12.1	2.3	9.6	62.9	2,572.7	2,649.3	−76.6
1987	110,222	20,417.3	5,398.5	7.7	2.3	5.4	114.5	2,713.4	3,215.1	−501.7
1988	99,839	20,869.7	4,783.9	−9.4	2.2	−11.4	1,722.3	2,719.9	2,865.1	−145.2
1989	86,431	21,319.9	4,054.0	−13.4	2.2	−15.3	2,775.3	3,503.3	2,286.5	1,216.8
1990	82,032	21,764.5	3,769.1	−5.1	2.1	−7.0	7,649.6	3,279.8	2,921.9	357.9
1991	83,760	22,203.9	3,772.3	2.1	2.0	0.1	139.2	3,393.1	3,595.3	−202.2
1992	83,401	22,640.3	3,683.7	−0.4	2.0	−2.3	56.7	3,578.1	4,001.4	−423.3
1993	87,375	23,073.2	3,786.9	4.8	1.9	2.8	39.5	3,384.7	4,160.4	−775.7
1994	98,577	23,502.0	4,194.4	12.8	1.9	10.8	15.4	4,424.1	5,499.2	−1,075.1
1995	107,064	23,926.3	4,474.7	8.6	1.8	6.7	10.2	5,491.4	7,732.9	−2,241.5

table continues next page

Table 2.4 National Accounts, 1973–2010 *(continued)*

	GDP	Population (thousands)	GDP per capita (S/. at 1994 prices)	Percent variation				US$ millions		
Year	(1)	(2)	(3)	(1)	(2)	(3)	Inflation	Exports of goods	Imports of goods	Trade balance
1996	109,760	24,348.1	4,507.9	2.5	1.8	0.7	11.8	5,877.6	7,864.2	−1,986.6
1997	117,294	24,767.8	4,735.7	6.9	1.7	5.1	6.5	6,824.6	8,535.5	−1,710.9
1998	116,522	25,182.3	4,627.2	−0.7	1.7	−2.3	6.0	5,756.8	8,218.7	−2,461.9
1999	117,587	25,588.5	4,595.3	0.9	1.6	−0.7	3.7	6,087.5	6,710.5	−623.0
2000	121,057	25,983.6	4,659.0	3.0	1.5	1.4	3.7	6,954.9	7,357.6	−402.7
2001	121,317	26,366.5	4,601.2	0.2	1.5	−1.2	−0.1	7,025.7	7,204.5	−178.8
2002	127,402	26,739.4	4,764.6	3.0	1.4	3.6	1.5	7,713.9	7,392.8	321.1
2003	132,545	27,103.5	4,890.3	4.0	1.4	2.6	2.5	9,090.7	8,204.8	885.9
2004	139,141	27,460.1	5,067.0	5.0	1.3	3.6	3.5	12,809.2	9,804.8	3,004.4
2005	148,640	27,810.5	5,344.7	6.8	1.3	5.5	1.5	17,367.7	12,081.6	5,286.1
2006	160,145	28,151.4	5,688.7	7.7	1.2	6.4	1.1	23,830.1	14,844.1	8,986.0
2007	174,407	28,481.9	6,123.4	8.9	1.2	7.6	3.9	28,094.0	19,590.5	8,503.5
2008	191,505	28,807.0	6,647.9	9.8	1.1	8.6	6.7	31,018.5	28,449.2	2,569.3
2009	193,155	29,132.0	6,630.3	0.9	1.1	−0.3	0.2	26,961.5	21,010.7	5,950.8
2010	210,143	29,460.7	7,133.0	8.8	1.1	7.6	2.1	35,564.8	28,815.3	6,749.5

Source: Data from Central Reserve Bank of Peru.

Table 2.5 Balance of Payments, 2000–10

US$ millions

	2000	2001	2002	2003	2004	2005	2006	2007	2008	2009	2010
I. Current account balance	−1,546	−1,203	−1,110	−949	19	1,148	2,872	1,460	−5,318	211	−2,315
1. Trade balance	−403	−179	321	886	3,004	5,286	8,986	8,503	2,569	5,951	6,750
a. Free-on-board exports	6,955	7,026	7,714	9,091	12,809	17,368	23,830	28,094	31,018	26,962	35,565
b. Free-on-board imports	−7,358	−7,204	−7,393	−8,205	−9,805	−12,082	−14,844	−19,591	−28,449	−21,011	−28,815
2. Services	−735	−963	−994	−900	−732	−834	−737	−1,192	−2,056	−1,144	−2,037
a. Exports	1,555	1,437	1,455	1,716	1,993	2,289	2,660	3,152	3,649	3,645	3,956
b. Imports	−2,290	−2,400	−2,449	−2,616	−2,725	−3,123	−3,397	−4,344	−5,704	−4,789	−5,993
3. Factor income	−1,410	−1,101	−1,457	−2,144	−3,686	−5,076	−7,562	−8,359	−8,774	−7,484	−10,053
a. Private	−896	−550	−746	−1,275	−2,715	−4,211	−6,883	−7,926	−8,888	−7,533	−9,873
b. Public	−513	−551	−711	−869	−970	−865	−679	−433	113	49	−180
4. Current account transfers	1,001	1,040	1,019	1,209	1,433	1,772	2,185	2,508	2,943	2,887	3,026
II. Financial account	1,023	1,544	1,800	672	2,154	141	348	8,400	8,674	1,499	12,921
1. Private sector	1,481	983	1,538	−105	937	1,818	2,166	8,809	9,509	2,680	13,324
2. Public sector	277	372	1,056	630	988	−1,441	−738	−2,473	−1,404	1,032	−1,004
3. Short-term capital	−735	189	−794	147	230	−236	−1,079	2,064	568	−2,214	601
III. Exceptional financing	−58	−1	14	64	26	100	27	67	57	36	19
IV. Net errors and omissions	388	110	129	689	151	239	−495	−272	−244	−702	566
V. Central Reserve Bank reserves flow (V = I + II + III + IV)	−192	450	833	477	2,351	1,628	2,753	9,654	3,169	1,043	11,192

Source: Data from Central Reserve Bank of Peru.
Note: Sums may not total because of rounding.

Figure 2.5 International Reserves, 1996–2011

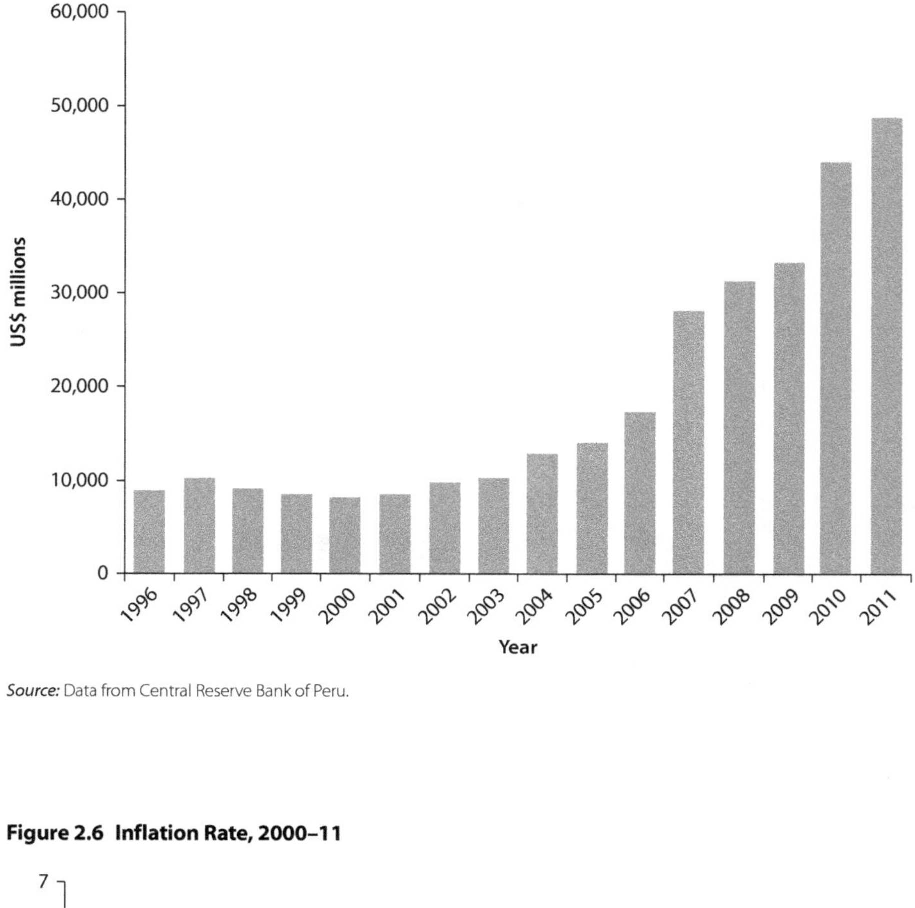

Source: Data from Central Reserve Bank of Peru.

Figure 2.6 Inflation Rate, 2000–11

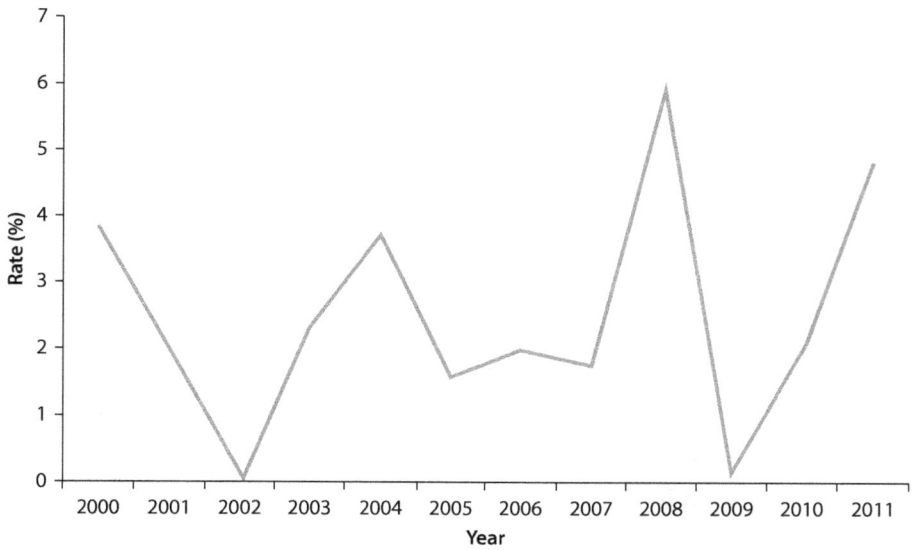

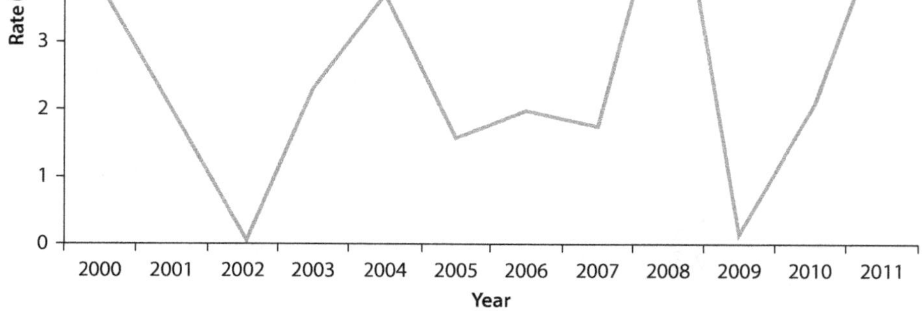

Source: Data from Central Reserve Bank of Peru.

Table 2.6 Nuevos Soles per U.S. Dollar Exchange Rate, 2000–10

	2000	2001	2002	2003	2004	2005	2006	2007	2008	2009	2010
Yearly average	3.490	3.508	3.518	3.479	3.414	3.297	3.275	3.129	2.926	3.012	2.830

Source: Data from Central Reserve Bank of Peru.

The president has the authority to appoint the policy makers. We consulted the agencies where the main policy makers on economy and finance work while preparing this chapter. Those agencies were the Ministry of Economy and Finance (Ministerio de Economía y Finanzas, or MEF), the Ministry of Foreign Commerce and Tourism (Ministerio de Comercio Exterior y Turismo, or MINCETUR), and the BCRP.

Analysis presented in *Fighting Fire with Fire* demonstrated that the government of Alberto Fujimori proceeded "to remove all the pieces of the protectionist scaffold, to subscribe to World Trade Organization (WTO) agreements, to create institutions to regulate free competition, and to decree the necessary rules" (Finger and Nogués 2006, 252) and that "liberalization was widely accepted as a way to advance the public interest, not simply as a desperate means to take on an economic crisis" (Finger and Nogués 2006, 21).

Ministry of Economy and Finance

According to the Organic Law and the Executive Power Law, MEF shall plan, lead, and control the matters related to the fiscal policy, funding, debt, budget, treasury, accounting, foreign commerce, and the policies of the financial business activity of the government, as well as harmonizing the economic activity.

MEF produces an annual document, the Multiannual Macroeconomic Framework (Marco Macroeconómico Multianual, or MMM), which presents its goals for economic policy, its impressions about the macroeconomic scenario of both the Peruvian economy and the global economy, and ways the government will use the instruments of economic policy to achieve its goals.[2]

If one reviews the MMMs issued in the first few years of the 2000–10 decade, one will find that MEF proposes the goal of achieving sustained growth at high rates. For this purpose, a constant increase of private investment is required to provide an increase of physical capital per worker, which will in turn improve productivity and increase competitiveness, thereby enabling Peru to expand its sales in international markets.

The MMM saw openness policies as fundamental to achieving these goals. The MMM of May 2003 (MEF 2003) proposes the following as part of the trade policy: "The Government shall continue implementing a trade policy strategy aimed at reducing the average tariff rates .... Peru endorses the establishment of new trade openness commitments." The free market is listed among the competition principles, highlighting the importance of "maintaining markets that are open to national and international free competition."

The MMM of 2004 goes a step further: the negotiation of bilateral and multilateral agreements to expand goods and services markets and to reduce the average tariffs is one of its main trade policy goals. The document also brings forward the need to manage tariff dispersion.

This treatment of trade in the annual MMM marked the beginning of a formal trade strategy that would bring together and extend the various steps that had been taken before. In the 1990s, business and government leaders spoke about "opening" as a natural reaction to the economic disaster that had occurred and brought forward public support for concrete steps, such as those previously described. The policy was basically to reduce tariffs and to push the private sector (both local and foreign-owned enterprises) to seek foreign markets. (Mining resources provided a solid base for foreign investment and exports.) Leaders, however, were careful not to give these reforms an ideological content; they particularly wanted to avoid bringing forward a strategy that might be interpreted as *rightist*.

Only when policy entrepreneurs were able to bring forward the real possibility of a successful FTA with the United States were they comfortable with adding an internationalist dimension to their reform strategy and with putting down in black and white the emerging elements of a policy structure. When Fernando Zavala Lombardi, whose management philosophy was present in INDECOPI (very transparent and careful with procedures), took office as minister of economy and finance, he moved boldly toward laying out a more complete strategy. Both the advancement of an FTA with the United States and the content of this strategy will be discussed later.

It was only in 2006, through the publication of Ministerial Resolution (Resolución Ministerial, or RM) 005-2006-EF/15, *Tariff Policy Guidelines*, that MEF presented a comprehensive document establishing a tariff policy as part of its global trade strategy (MEF 2005). This document is important not only because it establishes clear guidelines for a tariff policy, but also because, in approaching this matter, it develops concepts that imply the establishment of a development policy and a vision of the economic path the country needs follow.

Elements in the Trade Strategy

RM 005-2006-EF/15 establishes the unilateral liberalization of foreign commerce as the basic approach to tariff reform in that the tariff, as a tax applied only on imported goods, constitutes a protection bias. The resolution establishes that

> a balance will be made based on the potential effective impact—of tariffs—on the production, employment, or collection versus the efficiency in allocating resources and the well-being of the population.
>
> From an economic efficiency standpoint, tariff reduction promotes improvement in the international competitiveness of goods produced in the country and in the productivity of companies. It also allows for higher consumer satisfaction. The opposite, raising tariffs, isolates the economies from international competitiveness and benefits just a few sectors and groups in terms of income and employment, at the expense of the efficiency in the allocation of productive resources.
>
> Therefore, a useful policy design, particularly for a country with no influence over international prices (because it has a small economy) is reducing tariffs and,

> in so doing, reducing the distortion effect in the efficient allocation of resources, since such allocation will occur more in terms of the market, rather than due to the creation of artificial advantages.
>
> This argument is equally valid for the bills in the Congress of the Republic that aim to promote certain sectors through tariff exemptions that usually distort discretionary resource allocation. (MEF 2005, 2–3)
>
> There exist other means to achieve the goals of production, employment, or tax collection. Factors such as healthy macro-economic policies and policies—such as trade openness—that improve the country's competitiveness (better infrastructure, education, institutional character, among others) serve better the goals of widely creating employment and raising income in the medium and long term.
>
> **The direction that the multilateral, bilateral, and trade bloc negotiations are taking points to the elimination of tariffs as a policy instrument.** Tariff reduction within the framework of trade negotiation together with unilateral reductions will lead to the abolition of tariffs as a productive protection instrument and the substitution of tariff collection for another type of collection more based on taxes such as the general sales tax (IGV, in Spanish) or the income tax. In terms of relevance for Peru, this goal has to do with the trade negotiations carried out, currently in progress, or potential negotiations and their alignment to the WTO: the Free Trade Area of the Americas (FTAA); the free trade agreements (FTAs) with the United States, the European Union, or China; or economic enhancement agreements with countries of the region such as Mexico (MEF 2005, 2–3).

The Peru chapter in *Fighting Fire with Fire* explains that the government wanted "to institutionalize the trade policy decisions as well as install technical criteria and a unified evaluation system for protection requests" (Finger and Nogués 2006, 21). RM 005-2006-EF/15 lays out a rationale and a framework for making such changes.

In this way, MEF officials defined a long-term vision where economic development requires a correct allocation of resources based on market criteria and continuous improvement of the country's competitiveness. For this purpose, market openness (achieved through an openness policy) is an essential element.

Ministry of Foreign Commerce and Tourism

MINCETUR was created in 2002 to replace the Ministry of Industry, Tourism, and Commercial Negotiations. The change of name and the allocation of the industry sector to the current Ministry of Production occurred because the government wanted to grant due priority and relevance to trade policies and to separate them from whatever policies might be established to support industrial development. This change aligned the government agency responsible for the development and management of trade policy with those interests that were supportive of the vision of integrating Peru into the world economy as a key element in Peru's development policy.

Until 2002, Peru's participation in international agreements had played little part in the formation of Peru's trade policies. Peru was part of the Andean

Community of Nations (Comunidad Andina de Naciones, or CAN), an arrangement that came about with the signing of the Cartagena Agreement in 1969. The agreement was part of the import substitution strategy and policy then being followed by all founding members (Bolivia, Chile, Colombia, Ecuador, Peru, and República Bolivariana de Venezuela). Its purpose was to create a local market that was large enough to support local industries. As part of the agreement, each country would produce only preestablished lines of products, and imports would come only from the other members.

Little was achieved toward this objective. (CAN members took only 7 percent of the Peruvian exports in the 2000–10 decade, no more than before CAN was established.) Chile withdrew in 1976 as the country moved away from an import substitution strategy. As Peru has moved toward a strategy of integration into the global economy, and on the basis of market forces, the country has reduced many of its obligations in CAN. Peru no longer shares a development strategy with República Bolivariana de Venezuela, then under the leadership of Hugo Chávez, or with Bolivia, under the leadership of Evo Morales. Peru has remained a member of CAN mainly for diplomatic reasons. (CAN's headquarters is in Lima.) Colombia, which is also moving away from an import substitution strategy, has likewise stepped away from CAN as a vehicle for making economic policy.

As discussed in detail in *Fighting Fire with Fire*, Peru effectively used the WTO template for trade remedies in its reorganization of its mechanisms to manage domestic pressures for protection. This effort too was a unilateral action on the part of Peru and not a reform program that was conditional on changes negotiated with trading partners. Like most Latin American countries, Peru accepted ceiling rates tariff bindings at the Uruguay Round that were above the legal rates in Peru.[3]

In time, however, the possibility of negotiating an FTA with the United States entered into the array of instruments that reform leaders used to influence Peruvian trade politics and to propel Peruvian trade policy forward. Likewise, as Peru moved unilaterally to open its economy in the 1990s, the government also began to embrace other international agreements and to participate in their processes. This participation was intended to bring Peru's changing economic policies to the attention of other countries and to assure them that Peru intended to participate in and to abide by such agreements. Peruvian leaders, however, had no experience in the negotiating reciprocal concessions and worked from a realistic assessment of the power of a smaller economy to influence what big economies would give up in trade agreements.

Both the Peruvian business and government communities were active in broadening their links with their respective international communities. Peru, a signatory to the General Agreement on Tariffs and Trade since 1951, participated in the Uruguay Round negotiations and entered the WTO in 1995 as a charter member. Peru joined the Asia-Pacific Economic Cooperation (APEC), a nonbinding country forum, in 1998. Although Peru joined this forum for strategic reasons related to the country's return to the international financial orbit after the crisis of the 1980s, membership in APEC was an important milestone because it represented the first actual contact of both the Peruvian government and entrepreneurs in Peru with the government and business communities of the vast markets of the Asia-Pacific region. The Peruvian business community also expanded its links with the Pacific region through participation in the Pacific Basin Economic Council.[4] The Peruvian government had also been active in negotiations for the FTAA.

Andean Trade Preference Act

Peruvian leaders first took note of the possibility of using international negotiations as an effective part of their reforms when the Andean Trade Preference Act (ATPA) came up for renegotiation in 2001. The ATPA was first signed on December 4, 1991, during the administration of President Alberto Fujimori. In 2001, a new democratic government was in place; new people and new ideas were coming into the government. These leaders had 10 years of successful economic reform behind them and were ready for new goals.

Peruvian leaders recognized the need for the ATPA to continue. The FTAA negotiations were under way, but the most important agreement to drive Peruvian exports until then was the ATPA.

The ATPA was a unilateral decision made by the United States to offer certain Andean countries the reward of reduced tariffs on some products in exchange for cooperation in the war against drugs. In his book *Historia de un Desafío* (Story of a Challenge), Alfredo Ferrero (2010, 33), Peru's former minister of foreign commerce and tourism, describes the thoughts of the officers in charge of the trade policy at MINCETUR at that time. In regard to the need to create MINCETUR, he says:

> It was essential to create the conditions necessary to increase production aimed at added value exports, manufactured goods, and accessing various markets; … Such political intent had to translate itself into the creation of an agency in charge of the Government policies regarding foreign commerce which gathered the efforts of disperse entities providing stability, congruence, and ongoing presence in the task at hand.

In other words, capturing the potential offered by the ATPA would require an agency that would draw its support from those interests in Peru that were attracted by this potential. The existing ministry was structured toward those interests primarily concerned with maintaining their isolation from the global economy. Attempts to achieve something serious in trade through the existing ministry would be blocked by the interests that the ministry had traditionally served.[5]

The former minister of foreign commerce and tourism explains further in his book:

> This priority was established after a benchmark analysis between the GDP and the exports of various countries, with emphasis in those who had GDP and exports

> similar to Peru in 1970 (Taiwan[, China], [Republic of] Korea, etc.), and who, by the 2000s had increased their GDP significantly more than Peru due to an export development policy (Ferrero 2010, 32–33).

Ferrero notes that China had grown 194-fold by 2001, and Taiwan, China, had grown 96-fold. Meanwhile, Peru had grown only ninefold in that same period of 30 years.

This comparison with Asian countries was part of a report that Ferrero, then the vice minister, presented to Congress as part of his argument for the creation of MINCETUR; he needed to explain to Congress why foreign trade deserved a ministry of its own. At the time, the success story of the Asians was prominent in the minds of every interested official and entrepreneur, and these comparisons were effective in the case made to Congress for a new ministry.

In writing the book, Ferrero updated the comparisons:

> In 1970, [Republic of] Korea … and Taiwan[, China] exported about the same amounts as Peru … one billion dollars a year. Peru achieved record figures of 27.956 billion in 2007 …. In the meantime, [Republic of] Korea reached 386 billion dollars and Taiwan[, China], 345 billion dollars in 2007. (Ferrero 2010, 96)

Although the ATPA had a life of 10 years, it provided for triennial reviews of compliance. These reviews included the possibility of suspension of privileges. The need for the ATPA to be reconfirmed every three years was a condition that limited investments in the members' capacities to increase exports. In addition, the APTA did not cover industrial sectors, such as the textile industry. These hindrances and the vast opportunities that the U.S. market represents had an effect on policy makers' thinking not only as they were seeking an expansion for this tool, but also as they were considering the possibility of obtaining a much more ambitious deal.

Therefore, the ATPA was important not only for its intrinsic value but also for awakening the ambition of Peruvian officials to achieve a favorable entry to an enormous market. And its political value (the war against drugs) opened the doors of U.S. technocracy and bureaucracy to Peruvian officials.

With this background, a clear vision shared by the MINCETUR team emerged with regard to the path that the country needed to take——a vision of how Peru might move to expand its exports in global markets. At that time, this vision—the conquest of major markets by Peruvian exporters—seemed very ambitious and far from reach.

Thanks to the drive of Peruvian leaders, Congress was sufficiently taken with this vision that MINCETUR was established. Peru could move forward to take advantage of a very particular opportunity that opened in the first few years of the 2000–10 decade. Exploiting this opportunity would lead to the signing of a FTA with the United States, and this negotiation allowed Peruvian officials, in turn, to develop the experience necessary to negotiate other FTAs with other large economies.

We will review this process in detail later in the chapter.

Implementing the Long-Term Vision

Ministry of Economy and Finance

MEF officials had to consider several elements to implement the long-term vision they had established. With regard to the openness policy, two key components can be highlighted: (a) management of the tariff policy and (b) participation in the FTA negotiations.

Tariff Policy

As we described earlier, MEF established the goal of reducing the average rate and dispersion of tariffs. According to Peruvian law, tariffs are imposed, changed, or removed by the minister of economy and finance by a ministerial decree (*decreto supremo*) signed by him and the president. Hence, MEF has direct control of this issue.

The tariff reduction process started in the 1990s. In September 1990, the first big tariff change took place when fees were reduced to only three rates: 50 percent, 25 percent, and 15 percent. The average tariff of 66 percent, current in July 1990, was lowered to 26 percent (Boloña and Illescas 1997, 39, 52, 53). Throughout the decade, several attempts were made to establish a flat 15 percent tariff. A reduction schedule was published to achieve that goal. The resistance of the sectors producing for the local market prevented the application of this schedule (Boloña and Illescas 1997, 54).

The second significant change occurred in April 1997, when the new tariff ranges were regulated. Although only two tariff ranges of 12 percent and 20 percent were established, the inception of a 5 percent surcharge for some products resulted in four effective tariffs: 12 percent, 17 percent, 20 percent, and 25 percent.

Between 2000 and 2010, reduction of tariff rates and dispersion continued. Within this period, we can identify two distinct stages: (a) from 2000 until the end of 2005 and (b) from 2006 to 2010.The breaking point between these two stages was the approval of RM 005-2006-EF of January 2006 and RM 639-2006-EF of November 2006.

Before these resolutions were published, observers perceived that, although the goal of reducing tariffs remained, the form and the timeliness in the application of the changes did not seem to result from a comprehensive medium-term and long-term analysis but rather from a process with no apparent order—an arbitrary process. The minister in charge could decide at any moment to change a tariff, and he needed only to present a very simple ministerial decree to the president asking for his approval and signature.

For instance, in May 2002, Supreme Decree (*Decreto Supremo*, or DS) 047-2002-EF was approved, which reduced the tariff fees for some capital goods, hence creating a new tier of 7 percent. Including the application of surcharges, there were five tariff tiers: 7 percent, 12 percent, 17 percent, 20 percent, and 25 percent. Then, in April, a temporary 5 percent surcharge was created through DS 063-2002-EF for some products included in the 7 percent surcharge category. Therefore, in practice, these products returned to the previous 12 percent tier.

In September 2002, DS 135-2002-EF created a new 4 percent tariff for a series of pieces of machinery and equipment. According to unconfirmed information, the list of products subject to this tariff comprised machinery and equipment that were not manufactured in the country, something very difficult to verify. Peru then had a six-tier tariff system: 4 percent, 7 percent, 12 percent, 17 percent, 20 percent, and 25 percent.[6]

In February 2004, DS 031-2004-EF was published, which created a new 0 percent rate category. This new rate was to be applied to raw material, products, equipment, and machinery of the agricultural sector. According to unconfirmed information, this measure might have been part of a broader negotiation within the Council of Ministers that involved matters related to the FTA negotiations with the United States. Peru then had a seven-tier tariff system: 0 percent, 4 percent, 7 percent, 12 percent, 17 percent, 20 percent, and 25 percent.

Around the same time, supreme decrees were published that changed the fees for certain specific products, such as cigarettes (DS 119-2002-EF) or propane gas, butane gas, and petroleum gas (DS 079-2005-EF). Although these decrees did not entail a significant change in the average tariff, they reflected the lack of orderly management of the trade policy.

RM 005-2006-EF, *Tariff Policy Guidelines* (MEF 2005), and RM 639-2006-EF, *Guidebook for the Economic and Legal Analysis of Regulatory Production in MEF* (MEF 2006), were published to establish an order and improve the quality in the production of regulations in general (DS 649-2006-EF) and of tariff regulations in particular (DS 005-2006/EF).

As noted earlier, RM 005-2006-EF not only established a vision for a tariff policy but also lists a series of criteria to be taken into account when proposing tariff changes.

In this sense, the ministry resolution not only proposes a cost-benefit balance that takes into account the economy as a whole, but also introduces evaluation criteria for effective protection, for preventing trade diversion, for taking the terms and conditions of the agreements into account, and so forth.

RM 639-2006-EF sets forth a series of principles that must govern the regulatory policy of MEF, such as the principles of necessity, effectiveness, proportionality, transparency, and consistency. It also establishes prior assessment criteria for the economic effects of given measures and determines processes to propose, prepare, and approve a regulation. It includes a detailed manual of how the effects of any resolution issued by MEF have to be evaluated and describes the contents of the report that has to be prepared accordingly. Now a minister in charge cannot decide a tariff change without first ordering and preparing a report according to the standards established in RM 639-2006-EF. There are legal penalties for presenting a resolution for tariff change without preparing the required report. These regulations are the result of the efforts of MEF officials in charge of establishing a range of criteria for the creation of standards. In other words, MEF itself is aiming at improving governance.

By the end of 2005, the simple nominal tariff average had dropped to 10.2 percent according to the MMM of May 2005. In 2007 and 2008, DS 017-, 191-, 105-, 158-, and 163-2007-EF and DS 038-2008-EF were published. They not only reduced tariff fees further but did so by establishing an order for the tariff system in general. The 5 percent surcharges were abrogated. Therefore, by 2008, Peru had a tariff system of only three tiers: 0 percent, 9 percent, and 17 percent.

In 2010, DS 279-2010-EF reduced the fees to 0 percent, 6 percent, and 13 percent. And in 2011, DS 055-2011-EF reduced the 13 percent fee to 11 percent. Finally, the three-tier tariff system that is in effect now—0 percent, 6 percent, and 11 percent—was established.

The improvement in tariff work conducted by MEF is noticeable RM 005-2006-EF and RM 639-2006-EF were issued, because despite a few odd decrees—such as DS 119-2008-EF, which refers only to fluorescent lamps, and DS 062-2011-/EF, which refers to steel slag for safety glass manufacturing materials—a comprehensive effort has been carried out to reduce the tariffs in a homogeneous manner.

As annex 2A shows, the nominal average tariff dropped to 3.2 percent with 55.9 percent of the line items being at the 0 percent tier and only 10.5 percent of the line items being at the 11 percent tier (annex 2B). All capital goods are at the 0 percent tier and 74 percent of the total imports value is also at the 0 percent tier (annex 2B).

Participation in the FTA Negotiations

MEF officials played a very active role in the FTA negotiations, particularly in the negotiation of the FTA with the United States. That agreement was the most important one, not only because it was an agreement with the largest economy in the world and covered a broad scope of policies and practices, but also because it was the first such agreement being negotiated and would serve as a template for future negotiations.

According to the interviews conducted for this book, MEF had two main concerns about this negotiations program. First, MEF wanted to ensure that the terms and conditions of the agreements negotiated would entail no commitments from Peru that imposed standards that would slow the reform process in Peru. Moreover, MEF wanted to ensure that Peru did not accept any U.S. demands that would have the effect of compromising reforms already in place in Peru.

Second, MEF wanted to use the signing of the agreements as a locking process for reforms that Peru already had in place. Because the agreements constitute supranational commitments, they are relatively permanent; changing them legally, though possible, would be very difficult.

The 100 Decrees

Between March and June 2008, as the negotiations neared completion, the executive branch of government (of which MEF is part) asked Congress for the authority to issue decrees on a wide variety of matters deemed necessary to complete the implementation of the FTA with the United States. The authority, which Congress granted, would allow the executive branch to put in place reforms that they judged to be necessary and that went beyond the detail of what was required in the FTA. This authority was then the basis for the 100 legislative decrees described in this section.

MEF and MINCETUR were influential in the preparation of these decrees. They took advantage of the discretion contained in the grant of authority to implement what we could call second-generation reforms, including legislative decrees on matters not directly related to the implementation of the FTA or demanded by its terms.

As we review the list of decrees, we will find legislative decrees (*decretos legislativos*, or DLs) promoting national or foreign private investment in areas such as agricultural irrigation (DL 994), execution of social programs (DL 996), investment on rural electric systems (DL 1001), promotion of investment on electric power generation through the use of renewable energy (DL 1002), signing of legal stability agreements (DL 1011), the Framework Act of Public-Private Associations aimed at developing public infrastructure or providing utility services (DL 1012), and promotion of private investment in social housing construction projects (DL 1037, 1019, and 1020).

Other decrees aimed at achieving more efficiency in government management (DL 1017) and creating a new government contracting law (DL 1018). The decree dealing with central public procurement (DL 1022) modified the National Port System Act, and DL 1023 promoted private investment in the sector. Other decrees created the national authority of the civil service with respect to the government's human resource management system (DL 2024), created the public managers body (DL 1024), approved training regulations to evaluate government staff (DL 1025), and modified the General Finance System and Insurance Act incorporating the new Basel Agreement and the transparency principle (DL 1028). DL 1029 modified the Administrative Silence Act to speed up paperwork, and DL 1031 promoted efficiency in the government's entrepreneurial activity. DL 1035 created an act to conform to the agreement on investment measures related to trade as per WTO principles. DL 1038 created the Strategic Planning System, DL 1053 approved the new Customs General Law, DL 1061 modified the Stock Exchange Act, and DL 1063 approved the legislation on government goods acquisition through the commodity exchange. DL 1086 approved the Competitiveness Promotion Act for Small and Medium Industries.

Thus, in the course of the FTA negotiation process, MEF officials not only managed to attain their two main goals (achieving the locking process and avoiding the acquisition of commitments that entail a regression in the openness process) but also used the situation to advance the application of new legislation related to their development vision.

Ministry of Foreign Commerce and Tourism

Among the activities that MINCETUR officials had to carry out to achieve their long-term vision, the most relevant one was clearly the negotiation process for the FTA with the United States. Without a doubt, this negotiation has been one of the most important ones, if not the most important one, that has taken place in Peru's recent history. This assessment is based not only on the implementation of the terms of the agreement with the largest economy in the world or the complexity of the issues involved but also because it entailed an enormous effort by Peru's negotiating team. The negotiation required the implementation of very important reforms in the country's legal system. It also allowed Peru to acquire experience and a reputation for negotiation, which proved useful later when other important agreements were negotiated.

The history of the FTA negotiation process with the United States is very important, because after that process, most agents of the economy and civil society became involved in creating a national vision of the position Peru must achieve within the international market and the specific role that Peruvian companies and citizens could play in pursuing that goal.

FTA Negotiation with the United States

MINCETUR acknowledged that it would not have been able to succeed in negotiating the FTA without the assistance of important sectors of the government and the civil society, which met the challenge with determination. A dual agenda was thus prepared to achieve this goal. One agenda was prepared for the internal front, and another for the external front.

For the external front, the first challenge was placing Peru on the economic, political, and commercial radar of the United States. At the time, Peruvian exports represented less than 1 percent of U.S. imports. Peru was a little country in Latin America that had just emerged from a deep economic crisis and was timidly attempting to enter the global market. Hence, the Peruvian negotiating team had to find strategic areas that would be attractive to U.S. officials. For this purpose, the Peruvian negotiators found two small instruments, which they used very intelligently: (a) the interest of U.S. officials in the war against drugs and (b) the creation of the FTAA—a process that the United States was leading.

With regard to the war against drugs, starting a dialogue was within U.S. strategic interests, because Andean countries are the main producers of cocaine in the world. The main complaint of the Andean countries was that coca crops employed a significant sector of their economically active population. Therefore, the solution to this issue had to include an economic alternative to counteract the reduction of the coca crops. The ATPA had originated out of such concerns and was under consideration for renewal.

The ATPA renewal process allowed Peruvian officials to develop contacts and experiences that would prove to be important in the future FTA proposal. Many personal contacts were established with officials of the U.S. government and the U.S. Congress, including Cass Ballenger, Max Baucus, Philip Crane, Tom Daschle, Lincoln Diaz-Balart, Gary Edson, Bob Graham, Bennett Harman, Ted Kennedy, Carl Levin, Sander Levin, John McCain, Maria Pagan, Charles Rangel, William Thomas, and Robert Zoellick (Ferrero 2010, 68–72), as well as with negotiators from other Andean countries, including Ivonne Baki from Ecuador and Luis Alberto Moreno from Colombia. An ongoing communication with these officials confirmed their complete lack of knowledge of Peru—a situation that had to be resolved promptly.

A second matter that helped the Peruvians achieve their goal of signing an FTA with the United States was the faltering pace of the FTAA negotiations. These negotiations started in 1994, largely at the initiative of the United States, as an attempt to promote economic integration and also to create a political liaison mechanism with Latin America. Almost seven years of negotiations had not, however, made progress to resolve differences among Brazil, the United States, República Bolivariana de Venezuela, and the member states of MERCOSUR (the Common Market of the South, or Mercado Común del Sur) both within this forum and in other international forums. It was becoming apparent that reaching agreement was practically impossible.

Given that the FTAA negotiations were a U.S. initiative, their collapse would be an embarrassment for the U.S. government, and its relationship with the region might have been seriously affected. The U.S. government was anxious to prevent the perception of failure. The Andean forum countries—Colombia, Ecuador, and Peru—had been the most willing to achieve an agreement (and also to support the position of the United States in other forums such as the Group of 20). Thus, a significant change in the course of the negotiations occurred during the FTAA meeting in Miami at the end of 2003.The U.S. trade representative at that time, Robert Zoellick, announced the willingness of the United States to initiate FTA negotiations with Colombia, Ecuador, and Peru. The road was open for Peru.

In the negotiation of an FTA with the United States, bringing along the Peruvian business community and civil society—the internal front—entailed perhaps more and harder work than negotiating with the United States. However, the government had earlier laid the groundwork to take on such a challenge. As part of its negotiation of extension of the ATPA (which would be called the ATPEA, ATPA with the word *Expansion* added), the government had included the main business communities of the country in its efforts to join the global market.

President Fujimori took an important step toward involving the Peruvian business community by including its representatives in APEC meetings. Before Peru entered APEC, the Pacific Basin Economic Council had been created, led by Peruvian entrepreneur Gonzalo Garland. This forum consisted only of entrepreneurs and worked in alignment with APEC. Therefore, the efforts to join APEC started with coordination work among Peruvian entrepreneurs, who showed great interest in integrating Peru into the rest of the world.

In 2001, during the administration of President Alejandro Toledo (2001–06), a delegation led by Raúl Diez Canseco, who was then vice president of Peru, traveled to Washington, D.C., to promote the ATPEA. A group of government officials and Peruvian entrepreneurs were part of the delegation. The entrepreneurs were mainly from the textile sector, which had not been included in the ATPA. Ricardo Vega Llona, who was then the Peruvian antidrug czar, was also a member of the delegation. He had previously chaired the National Confederation of Private Business Associations, an association of the most important business associations of the country.

The goal of including entrepreneurs in the delegation was "to send a signal to the American officers and Congressmen that the Peruvian government worked in favor of industry and job creation, so that the lack of jobs would not lead Peruvians toward illegal coca crops and drug trafficking" (Ferrero 2010, 71). The president at that time, Alejandro Toledo, wanted entrepreneurs to become acquainted with the dynamics of negotiations in the U.S. Congress.

After the approval of the ATPEA in 2002, MINCETUR gave official recognition and separate standing to its U.S. division. This small group in the ministry was led by Eduardo Ferreyros, who had been in charge of all matters related to the United States. Ferreyros worked for MINCETUR from1999 until 2011, when he was appointed minister of foreign commerce and tourism.

Eduardo Ferreyros recounts that, although most business groups were in favor of the FTA, some had reservations and others were against it. For instance, the National Society of Industries sent a communication to MINCETUR after the approval of the ATPEA expressing its opposition. The communication stated that given the fact that Peru had an exports promotion tool such as the ATPEA, there was no need for an FTA (Ferrero 2010, 77). Therefore, MINCETUR started a campaign to inform entrepreneurs about the benefits of the FTA in an effort to gain their total support.

The MINCETUR negotiating team proposed that Peruvian entrepreneurs hold working sessions to listen to the concerns of all productive sectors with regard to all the matters subject to negotiation. The condition for carrying out those meetings was that MINCETUR would be the only spokesperson in charge of informing the public of the progress and status of the negotiations. All participants were asked to sign a confidentiality agreement and to organize groups for each of the 21 parallel tables of the negotiation:

- Access to markets (industry)
- Access to markets (textile)
- Customs procedures
- Origin rules
- Technical barriers to trade
- Agriculture
- Sanitary and phytosanitary measures
- Financial services
- Cross-border services
- Telecommunications
- Electronic commerce
- Investments
- Public procurement
- Competition policies
- Safeguards
- Labor affairs

- Environment
- Controversy resolution
- Institutional affairs
- Intellectual property
- Skill building

The transparency and the design of this process attracted the attention and trust of the majority of the participants, which facilitated the establishment of a partnership with the private sector and a commitment to the chosen course of action. Hence, even those who had initially opposed the project were convinced that it was the best course for the country.

The Peruvian entrepreneurs responded in concert by creating the Business Council for International Negotiations, a coordinating agent with the government. The council was formed by National Confederation of Private Business Associations, the National Society of Industries, the Foreign Commerce Society of Peru, the Exporters Association, the Chamber of Commerce of Lima, and the chambers of commerce of the main cities of Peru, among other entrepreneur unions.

The efforts of MINCETUR went beyond summoning the entrepreneurial sector. They aimed at involving the whole civil society. The first surveys indicated that only 25 percent of the population approved of the FTA negotiation, whereas the vast majority was against it, recounts Eduardo Ferreyros. Given the low approval rate and the population's lack of knowledge about the benefits of the FTA with the United States, MINCETUR started an ambitious communication program that involved presentations, forums, and discussion groups about the convenience of a trade agreement. In this context, approximately 600 presentations were conducted throughout the country. About 50 percent of the informational meetings took place outside of Lima.

These meetings had the participation of trade unions, labor unions, chambers of commerce, universities, professional associations, farming communities, and communities involving other productive sectors, such as fishing. Other events were held, such as institutional events. These processes engaged up to 28 public institutions, so that the FTA "gradually became the 'mandatory subject' for various institutions and conference organizers" (Ferrero 2010, 78).

An encompassing process opened up for Peru. MINCETUR officials, together with a significant sector of the civil society, began a negotiation process under the assumption that the best course for developing the Peruvian economy was its integration with the largest economy in the world, not only through the liberalization of trade but also through integration of other aspects of the economy, such as respect for intellectual property and environmental, administrative, and labor matters, among others.

President Toledo opted for a strong leadership to ensure the success of the negotiations and gave his full support to the negotiating team, which he expressed in the following comment: "This FTA will be signed no matter what; otherwise my name will no longer be Alejandro Toledo" (Ferrero 2010, 159).

By the end of 2005, and after countless obstacles on both the internal and the external fronts were overcome, the negotiations were finally completed. On December 7, a ceremony in Washington, D.C., marked the closing of negotiations. By then, the plan to gain the support of the Peruvian public had proved to be successful. According to new surveys, the initial skepticism had been overcome, and 75 percent of the people surveyed were in favor of signing an FTA with the United States.

As Peru went through its presidential and congressional election campaigns, Congress took up the approval of the FTA. The new administration was to take office on July 28, 2006. During the election campaign, Alan García Pérez, who later won the election, had criticized the FTA and had announced the review of the agreement: "If he (referring to Toledo) dares to sign the agreement, I shall erase his signature so that it is discussed by the whole country" (Ferrero 2010, 297).

On June 29, 2006, the government received Congress's approval of the FTA. The president-elect and the newly elected members of Congress had not yet taken office. However, Peru would have to wait until 2007 for approval by the U.S. Congress, since its composition had changed after the U.S. congressional election in November 2006.

After the election, it became evident that candidate García's previous position on the FTA and generally with regard to the trade openness reflected only an electoral strategy. According to Mercedes Aráoz, minister of foreign commerce and tourism under García, in a cabinet meeting soon after García took office, the president said, "We have to ride the wave of global economic growth not only by attempting to enter that market, but also by attracting investments and approaching those countries that have big markets and the highest growth rates."[7]

In a book published after he completed his 2001–06 term as president, *Against the Economic Fear: Believing in Peru*, García stated his strong support for Peru's emerging trade policy: "Free trade agreements have been signed with the United States, China, [Republic of] Korea, Singapore, the European Union, Japan, Chile, Mexico, the European Free Trade Area (EFTA), among others. As a result, we have reached 2.5 billion consumers" (García Pérez 2011, 143).

Political support for uniting Peru with the global economy had become widespread. In addition to the stances elaborated by political leaders, there were a number of more subjective indicators. For instance, through several opinion surveys, the government had learned that many small and medium-size entrepreneurs aspired to become exporters. A former minister of trade described this aspiration as the *sueño dorado* (golden dream) of smaller business. Small and medium-size enterprises are very important in Peru because they represent a big portion of the employment and of the GDP in general. Their willingness to become exporters suggests that this attitude is the result of the openness policy, which has helped their businesses prosper.

As the FTA negotiations progressed, Peruvian negotiators developed technical indicators to guide their positions (for example, tariff criteria to ensure that the result was trade creation rather than trade diversion). The negotiating team's objective was to use the negotiations to help reduce barriers in such a way as to generate more global trade.

Politically, the intent was not only to improve the image of Peru globally, but also to confirm Peru's position as a country that was fully committed to the global economic integration. MINCETUR, the Ministry of Foreign Affairs, and MEF constitute a unified team that continues to pursue this goal. The team has represented Peru actively in other global forums, such as APEC and the Cairns Group (a coalition of countries within the WTO that works toward openness in agricultural matters). President García Pérez (2011, 143–44) commented that in international meetings such as those of APEC, "now Peru is seen with respect; it is no longer seen the way it was ten years ago."

After completing the agreement with the United States, García instructed government officials not only to finalize and complete the negotiations of the FTA with the United States but also to continue with the negotiations of other FTAs initiated in the previous administration, such as the FTAs with Chile, Singapore, and Thailand. In addition, the government initiated negotiations for FTAs with China, the European Union, Japan, the Republic of Korea, and the EFTA. The government also moved to expand the economic enhancement agreements with MERCOSUR and Mexico.

Implementation of the U.S. FTA: A "Second Generation" of Reform

Before the FTA between Peru and the United States was approved in the United States, elections there had shifted political control, and the U.S. Congress insisted that some aspects of the FTA be renegotiated. Had the Peruvian executive branch of government been tepid in its support for the new trade philosophy, it might have seen this delay as an opportunity to slow the liberalization process in Peru. It chose the opposite course and moved quickly to ask the Peruvian Congress for authorization to undertake reforms on the new subjects that the United States raised. As noted earlier, the government submitted more than 100 supreme decrees to the Congress for approval between March and June 2008. They covered not only the subjects required to meet the terms of the FTA negotiation, but also other subjects that constituted a kind of second-generation reform that would prepare Peru for participation in the global market. This set of supreme decrees included such matters as a new customs law to conform to the U.S. standard; a public-private association law, through which private companies could propose the development of projects that the government would undertake; and a new public companies act, which would permit government-owned companies to be listed on the Lima Stock Exchange but would also subject them to the transparency regulations of the stock market on the same basis as the private companies listed there. These second-generation reforms also included creation of the Ministry of the Environment and a revision and extension of the INDECOPI law. INDECOPI is discussed later in this chapter.

Table 2.7 Main Economic Agreements

Country or group of countries	*Type of agreement*	*Signature date*	*Effective date*
United States	Free trade agreement	April 12, 2006	February 1, 2009
European Union	Free trade agreement	March 23, 2011	March 1, 2013
China	Free trade agreement	April 28, 2009	March 1, 2010
Japan	Free trade agreement	May 31, 2011	March 1, 2012
Korea, Rep.	Free trade agreement	March 21, 2011	August 1, 2011
Canada	Free trade agreement	May 29, 2008	August 1, 2009
Singapore	Free trade agreement	May 29, 2008	August 1, 2009
European Free Trade Area (Iceland, Liechtenstein, Norway, and Switzerland)	Free trade agreement	June 24, 2010 (European Free Trade Area states); July 14, 2010 (Peru)	July 1, 2011[a]
Mexico	Free trade agreement	April 6, 2011	February 1, 2012
Chile	Free trade agreement	August 22, 2006	March 1, 2009
Thailand	Free trade agreement	November 2010	December 31, 2011
Other trade agreements			
Switzerland	Agreement on agriculture	July 14, 2010	July 1, 2011
Norway	Agreement on agriculture	July 14, 2010	Not yet in force
Iceland	Agreement on agriculture	July 14, 2010	Not yet in force
Agreements under negotiation			
Guatemala	Free trade agreement		
El Salvador	Free trade agreement		
Honduras	Free trade agreement		

Source: Data from Ministry of Foreign Commerce and Tourism.
Note: Countries are listed by value of Peruvian exports affected.
a. Regarding the Confederation with Switzerland and the Principality of Liechtenstein.

By the end of Alan García's administration, Peru had signed FTAs with Canada, Chile, China, the European Union, Japan, Korea, Mexico, Singapore, Thailand, and the United States (table 2.7).

These results were possible only because of the dedicated and outstanding work of many government officials. The new democratic regimes of 2001–11 were capable not only of convoking many of the best professionals but also of giving them the continuity to develop very important goals. Following are a few examples of the highly qualified professionals who served the country during an important period:

- Fernando Zavala Lombardi, general manager of INDECOPI, 1995–2000; adviser to MEF, 2001–02; vice minister, MEF, 2002–05; minister, MEF, 2005–06.
- Javier Illescas, 26 years as a public official; area chief of international economy and macroeconomic analysis at the BCRP; economic adviser to MINCETUR and MEF; general director of the International Economy, Competitiveness and Private Investment Office, MEF; chief negotiator for MEF on the financing

services chapter of the FTA with the United States; MEF representative in negotiations for several agreements, including WTO, FTAA, APEC, CAN, and various FTAs.

- Alfredo Ferrero Diez Canseco, vice minister, MINCETUR, 1999–2003; minister, MINCETUR, 2003–06.
- Eduardo Ferreyros Kuppers, MINCETUR adviser on APEC forum, 1999–2000; official in charge of bilateral trade issues with the United States and general coordinator of FTA negotiations with the United States, MINCETUR, 2000–07; vice minister, MINCETUR, 2007–10; minister, MINCETUR, 2010–11.

Negotiation and Implementation: Making Things Happen

Negotiating the FTA with the United States

We have described the scope and results of the FTA negotiations. The progression from idea to result was not without problems. In this section, we describe some of those problems and explain what Peruvian officials did to overcome them. During the FTA negotiations with the United States, MINCETUR officials faced various problems on both the internal and the external fronts. The main problem on the external front was Peru's lack of visibility internationally, which could render a negotiation with the country unattractive for U.S. officials. Earlier, we detailed how the MINCETUR officials successfully dealt with this limitation.

On the internal front, the FTA negotiation with the United States was a delicate political process. Probably the most significant internal problem was the lack of public approval regarding the signing of the agreement. As we saw earlier, when the government made public its decision to negotiate an FTA with the United States, surveys indicated that only 25 percent of the population favored such negotiation. The high levels of disapproval became manifest through various mobilizations and sit-ins (which were silent protests) that generally took place in front of the MINCETUR offices. As we saw, this problem was gradually and completely resolved through a very important communication program launched by MINCETUR, which included more than 600 presentations throughout the nation.

Sector-related problems also arose, the most critical sectors being agriculture, pharmaceuticals, and textiles.

The Ministry of Agriculture was in charge of communicating the serious concerns of various business and labor organizations to the government. The main concern was that the U.S. agricultural sector would affect the Peruvian food market because, as is well known, the U.S. government grants several subsidies to this sector.

The complaints focused mainly on three products: wheat, cotton, and corn. The draft agreement proposed to reduce the tariffs on these products of American origin to 0 percent, though leaving in place the import tariffs for the same products from other countries. At one point, according to our sources, MEF suggested providing monetary compensation to the affected producers as the FTA was implemented.

Although the tariff was being negotiated by the team from MINCETUR, tariff policy was in fact in the hands of MEF. MEF had a program in place to reduce all tariffs unilaterally. (Overall, this program enjoyed widespread support within the government.) MEF had in reserve an inventory of tariff reduction decrees and would propose them to the president only when the ministry thought it opportune. In time, MEF, under its program, reduced these rates to zero on a most-favored-nation basis, thereby taking those rates out of the FTA negotiations. MEF was not called on to implement its previous suggestion for monetary compensation.

With regard to the pharmaceutical sector, the Peruvian entrepreneurs were mainly concerned with the possible inclusion of second-use patents for pharmaceutical products, which would seriously affect the sales of generic products manufactured in Peru. To resolve this problem, the negotiating team was committed to and achieved excluding these patents from the FTA.

For the textile sector, the entrepreneurs' main concern had to do with imports of footwear and used apparel. This matter was resolved in a similar way by excluding the imports of these used products, as set forth by Peruvian domestic legislation.

Negotiating the FTA with China

Peruvian officials negotiated an FTA with China (in force since March 1, 2010) in an effort to open the vast Chinese market to Peruvian exports. The commercial exchange between China and Peru had gone from a little over US$734 million in 2000 to US$10.575 billion in 2010. In 2009, China became Peru's second most important commercial partner, after the United States.

An important objective for China was to achieve recognition by Peru as a market economy for purposes of application of antidumping measures under the WTO antidumping agreement. Argentina, Brazil, and Chile had already so recognized China, and recognition by Peru would be another step in regularizing such treatment under the WTO.

The main obstacle for signing this agreement was the fear among entrepreneurs of the potential effect of Chinese exports in the Peruvian market after the approval of the agreement, keeping in mind not only the enormous amount of subsidies and other aid provided by the Chinese government to Chinese companies, but also events in Brazil, which faced huge problems after it declared China a market economy.

In this sense, the Peruvian negotiators took significant precautions during the negotiation. The first precautionary measure was to exclude a number of tariff items from the FTA.[8] This list included 592 tariff items representing 5 percent of the lines in the Peruvian tariff.

In this regard, Eduardo Ferreyros, the minister of foreign commerce and tourism, stated that before negotiations between the countries began, a joint feasibility study was conducted to identify sectors that would potentially benefit from, as well as sectors that might be sensitive to, the negotiation. That study found that some products of the textile-apparel sector, leather and footwear, and some products from the metal-mechanic industry might be affected by a tariff reduction with China.

A *D-basket*, or *excluded basket*, was added to the negotiation procedure to address these sensitivities. Products on which tariffs would not be reduced would be placed in the basket during the negotiation process. In the beginning, Peru requested the exemption of a large number of items that jointly represented 13 percent of its trade with China. China's position was that no more than 10 percent could be exempted if the FTA was to be validated by the WTO. According to Ferreyros, "We held meetings with the Peruvian private sector to see how we would reduce the list from 13 percent of trade to 10 percent of trade, and the joint work resulted in the list of items of the D-basket."[9] Ferreyros explained that achieving China's agreement in exempting the main lines in the footwear and textile-apparel sector was very difficult. China had significant interests as an exporter in those sectors and, therefore, wanted the sectors to benefit from the agreement.

Ferreyros further explained that MINCETUR initially planned the inclusion of more tariff items on the *no reductions* list, but the list had to include a minimum number of tariffs because of a WTO requirement establishing the trade percentage rate that needed to be included in a bilateral agreement.

The second precautionary measure was to include a bilateral safeguard in section 6 of the agreement that allows the possibility of implementing provisional safeguard measures. The negotiation of such a bilateral safeguard provision was influenced by the previous application of safeguards against imports from China. In 2003, the government ordered a safeguard investigation for apparel from China that included 106 tariff items, and provisional safeguards were imposed. That investigation was established pursuant to the document of accession of China to the WTO.

After the 200 days set forth as the maximum allowed term for provisional transition safeguards, and because of the pressure from the Chinese government, the Peruvian government opted to transform this procedure into a general safeguards procedure, under the WTO safeguard agreement, but only for 20 tariff items. Compared with the previous procedure, this one had two main differences: (a) the number of line items and (b) the fact that the general safeguards under the WTO safeguard agreement are for imports of any origin, unlike transition safeguards under the Chinese protocol of accession, which could be applied exclusively to items of Chinese origin. Provisional taxation was imposed, which was maintained only during the 200 days allowed by the WTO agreement. Since injury had not by that time been determined, the government lifted the provisional measures and terminated the investigation.

The third precautionary measure was the inclusion of DS 004-2009-PCM in the national legislation. This decree modifies DS 006-2003-PCM, which regulates the standards set forth in the agreement with regard to the application of article VI of the General Agreement on Tariffs and Trade of 1994 (which deals with antidumping). Article 6 of this decree, "Calculation of the normal value and dumping margin for special cases," allows the calculation of the dumping margin "with a comparable price of a similar product when this product is exported to a third appropriate country ... or with the production cost in the country of origin plus a reasonable amount on account of administrative expenses, sales expenses, and general expenses, as well as benefits" when there is a special market situation. A *special market situation* is defined as the situation that arises when production costs, including inputs, services, or trade and distribution expenses, are distorted.

In this way, INDECOPI authorities are granted greater flexibility in calculating dumping values in cases where the local Chinese market attempts to use a distorted normal value. The Subsidies and Dumping Control Committee of INDECOPI has invoked the application of this article in most cases of dumping against China.

Lastly, a special customs agreement was negotiated with China. This agreement sets forth a series of procedures for information and control between the customs authorities of the two countries in an attempt to prevent the biggest problem created by Chinese exports: undervaluation. Indeed, a significant flow of exports at negligible prices from multiple Chinese companies had been observed in recent years. These imports not only affected local Peruvian manufacturers but also prevented the Peruvian tax authority from collecting the tariffs and the general sales tax corresponding to the actual value of imports.

The customs agreement aims at avoiding, controlling, and prosecuting this type of informal trade. We have been informed that, on finishing this document, the Peruvian authorities requested specific information from Chinese authorities on the practices of certain exporters. Peruvian authorities accepted that the information collected would be deemed confidential as the agreement itself sets forth. We could not confirm whether the response to this request has been satisfactory.

The objective of these precautionary measures was to provide instruments through which the Peruvian government could prevent abuse by Chinese exporters in sectors where a national industry existed.

Summary Comparison of the FTAs with the United States and China

FTA with the United States

Although the MINCETUR officials' primary goal was to open the markets of the richest country in the world to Peruvian exports, in practice the negotiation included many other political and economic matters.

The final text of the agreement comprises 23 chapters and includes subjects such as the following: customs administration and trade facilitation, public hiring, investment, competition policies, designated monopolies and government companies, telecommunications, intellectual property rights, labor, environment, and transparency.[10] These matters go beyond the mere trade of goods and services. As we have mentioned, this list includes matters that MEF officials considered essential for the locking process of the reforms.

In every bilateral negotiation, it is customary to first negotiate the matters to be included in the agreement. The inclusion of many of the matters highlighted in the previous paragraph might have been proposed by the United States because they are of interest not only to the U.S. government but also with respect to the Bipartisan Agreement on Trade Policy developed by leaders of the Republican and the Democrat Parties in the U.S. Congress.

The Office of the U.S. Trade Representative's website states the following: "The PTPA [FTA] eliminates tariffs and removes barriers to U.S. services, provides a secure, predictable legal framework for investors, and strengthens protection for intellectual property, workers, and the environment. The PTPA is the first agreement in force that incorporates groundbreaking provisions concerning the protection of the environment and labor rights that were included as part of the Bipartisan Agreement on Trade Policy developed by Congressional leaders on May 10, 2007."[11]

Indeed, the FTA includes a long chapter on property rights (chapter 16), in which the parties commit to adhere to a long list of treaties related to copyrights, patents, trademarks, and so forth. This chapter contains comprehensive details on the procedures to register trademarks, Internet domains, copyrights, satellite carrier signals, patents, and intellectual property rights. In this way, Peru has adapted its legislation to conform with the most current requirements.

With regard to investments (chapter 10), the parties commit to treat the companies of the other country in no less favorable terms than those by which they treat the companies of their own country. Chapter 10 establishes the protection conditions against expropriation, except for explicit reasons in article 10.7, as well as an indemnification regime for the latter. It ensures the free flow of monetary transfers related to the investments of each party and a detailed controversy resolution system that allows access to the various arbitration courts, such as the International Centre for Settlement of Investment Disputes, the United Nations Commission on International Trade Law, or any other institution that has been mutually agreed on. This procedure allows for an arbitration process in case one of the parties imposes measures that can be deemed expropriatory. In this way, Peru ratified the existing legislation and promoted foreign investments, as well as nondiscriminatory treatment of investments, regardless of their origin.

Chapter 17 describes in detail the labor commitments, including not only the acknowledgment of the obligations the parties have as members of the International Labour Organization but also, specifically, the elimination of any form of forced or mandatory labor, the effective abolition of child labor, and the elimination of discrimination in employment and occupation. The parties established the Labor Affairs Council, which, among other functions, supervises the implementation of the chapter on labor and reviews its advancement. This chapter also includes—at Peru's request—a mechanism for labor cooperation and skill building to promote development and increase job opportunities.

Chapter 18 describes the rights related to an optimal use of environmental resources in compliance with the goal of sustained development. For this purpose, the Environmental Affairs Council was established. This council ensures the implementation of this chapter. It also ensures that all the information regarding environmental legislation will be made available to the public.

With regard to other subjects related to trade defense, the FTA states in chapter 8 that the antidumping and antisubsidy procedures that might occur between the United States and Peru will be strictly governed pursuant to the regulations established by the WTO.

With regard to safeguards, the agreement states that for global safeguards, the parties will apply such measures pursuant to the provisions of the WTO. It also allows the application of a bilateral safeguard for a transition period.

In this way, Peru consolidates a qualitative advance in its regulations by committing to maintain a very advanced legislation on such important matters. Supranationally, Peru commits to enforce this regulation so that it may not unilaterally withdraw from these commitments without breaching international treaties that have the force of national law under the Peruvian constitution. The process for breaching a treaty would have to be initiated by the executive power and would be very visible and public. Constitutionalists maintain that a change in a treaty requires the same procedures as a change in the constitution (which may require a referendum or a two-thirds majority in Congress for two years in a row). Moreover, a citizen whose interests are compromised by the Peruvian government's departing from the terms of such a treaty (without formally rescinding the treaty) could defend those interests against the government's actions through the Constitutional Tribunal.

FTA with China

The agreement with China resembles more a simple commercial treaty.[12] The majority of its 200 articles refer to commercial matters exclusively, such as lists of products, tax credit schedules, origin rules, and customs procedures.

The agreement contains four subjects that are not related solely to international trade. These chapters refer to investment, intellectual property, cooperation, and transparency. According to our sources, these subjects were included at the request of the Peruvian negotiators. The chapter on investments (chapter 10) was requested to facilitate Peruvian companies' participation in China, because such participation may require very complex paperwork for some sectors. The chapter on intellectual property (chapter 11) is basically a very brief approach to that subject and is only three pages long. Chapter 12, on cooperation, was designed so that various Peruvian agencies could have access to the comprehensive cooperation programs run by the Chinese government. The chapter on transparency (chapter 13) aims at guaranteeing an understanding of the extensive Chinese regulations, which have been used quite unexpectedly to impede or delay the entrance of Peruvian products.

With regard to trade defense matters, chapter 5 of the FTA states that any antidumping and subsidies activities that might occur between China and Peru, as in the case of the FTA between Peru and the United States, will be governed in strict compliance with the provisions set forth by the WTO. The same applies in the case of global safeguards. As in the FTA with the United States, the agreement also provides for a bilateral safeguard measure for a transition period.

The difference in scope of the two agreements is clear. For China, the main goal of the agreement was to achieve the political declaration of a market economy by Peru. This declaration is very important for China as a WTO member with restrictions. China seeks to eliminate these restrictions through the political support of as many member states of the WTO as possible. For Peru, the most important aspect of the agreement with China is achieving freer entrance of Peruvian products to the Chinese market. As a result of the experience gained in previous negotiations, Peru achieved the additional guarantees we have described.

The motivation for the agreement with the United States was very different. On the one hand, the United States negotiators wanted to ensure that Peruvian competition took place within the framework of social, labor, and environmental obligations, among others, that applies to U.S. companies. On the other hand, the agreement helped policy makers in Peru to advance the case for integration into the global economy. The agreement helped to inspire confidence in the Peruvian business community and civil society and demonstrated that Peruvians were as able as the citizens of any other country to prosper in a globally competitive environment.

Other Examples of Good Governance Practices

National Institute for the Defense of Competition and the Protection of Intellectual Property

Throughout this book, we have been able to confirm the improvement in governance that took place in the past decade, both for MEF and MINCETUR, and the beneficial effects it had on the Peruvian economy. This section takes up the role of INDECOPI, the government organization created as the centerpiece of constructive management of microeconomic regulation, of which the management of trade remedies was an important part. This organization can serve as an example for other countries.

As we saw in *Fighting Fire with Fire* (Finger and Nogués 2006), when it was founded in 1993, INDECOPI had a design and a way of working that were quite novel for a government institution in Peru at that time. INDECOPI's work is based on committees and autonomous councils formed by independent experts in the areas of defense of competition, consumer protection, intellectual property, and so forth. These experts act as judges in arbitrating conflicts in their jurisdiction. The committees have been successful because they have been able to summon professionals with a high level of technical experience and because their officials have had a very well-defined vision of the institution's goals as an arbitrator and promoter of a market economy in Peru (Finger and Nogués 2006, 254).

Jaime Thorne León, the head of INDECOPI from 2006 to 2010, says, "The creation of INDECOPI goes together with the openness of the Peruvian economy into a market economy. For this [to occur], there [have] to be institutions in place to monitor and control what is going on in the market." Thorne comments that, while attending various international forums representing INDECOPI, many specialists commented to him not only that INDECOPI was a unique agency in the world, but also that, in their opinion, the head of INDECOPI had a lot of power. Thorne has a very clear answer to this last comment: "Indeed, the head of INDECOPI has a lot of power, but once the committees and the councils are appointed, this power is immediately transferred to these instances, since the decisions they make do not require the approval of the head of INDECOPI."[13]

The organizational chart of INDECOPI states that the chair has a Consultative Committee. To this committee, the chair proposes a set of three specialists for each committee and council. The Consultative Committee then recommends the appointment of the most suitable people for each committee and council. This appointment system allows the members of the committees and councils to have the best technical and professional profile.

The Consultative Committee, in turn, is appointed by the Council of Ministers. Individuals summoned for the Consultative Committee have great personal and professional prestige and have independence with regard to political power. For instance, under Thorne's presidency, the Consultative Committee comprised a renowned professor of the most prestigious Peruvian university, a distinguished former judge and historian, a noted lawyer who is a former chair of the Bar Association of Lima, a very important entrepreneur, a former president of the National Confederation of Private Business Associations, a former chair of INDECOPI, and a noted entrepreneur specializing in small and medium-size companies.

Conversely, the president and the board of directors appoint the personnel of the technical secretary offices and the administrative personnel in charge of providing technical and administrative support to the investigations needed for each case.

INDECOPI now has the collaboration of approximately 1,000 people. And thanks to the appointment process and the clear vision proposed by the agency, it performs very well. INDECOPI is frequently listed as one of the three most approved government agencies. Thorne highlights the fact that this approval is particularly significant if one considers that INDECOPI acts as an arbitrator between two or more parties in the resolution of conflicts, whereas other highly approved agencies, such as the National Registry of Identification and Civil Status (the agency in charge of issuing national identity cards) or the BCRP, do not have conflict resolution between individuals and companies as part of their daily duties.

The fact that a single agency gathers authorities and professionals who work together on controlling, regulating, and defending the way the market works on a daily basis and who deal with vastly different matters (for example, competition, intellectual property, and consumer protection) allows for constant feedback among the professionals involved. This coexistence results in continuous improvement and greater sophistication of the agency's practices while working in a pro-market environment that constantly consults various areas, allowing it to develop sound jurisprudence.

INDECOPI's organizational model has a clear separation of powers. It allows INDECOPI to work better than other regulating agencies. For example, in the Supervisory Agency of Investments in Public Transportation Infrastructure and the Supervisory Agency of Private Investments in Telecommunications, a huge amount of decision-making power is concentrated in one person, the president of the agency.

INDECOPI's success with regard to clear, predictable technical management in conflict resolution has established an important role model for how a public or private agency should work in Peru. Because of its prestige and the fact that its processes take place in an orderly manner and that the decisions are made by specialized councils, rarely has any other government or private organization challenged its competence in conflict resolution. Hence, the perception is that INDECOPI processes are technical and not political. Attempting to dispute INDECOPI's area of competence would have a negative effect on public opinion. Moreover, in many cases of social conflicts, other political authorities request INDECOPI's participation as a guarantee of impartial management of the conflict.

As discussed in chapter 4, Global Trade Alert data (in table 4.1) show that all import control measures taken in Peru have been formal in nature, meaning that formal antidumping, antisubsidy, or safeguard processes are in place. According to Global Trade Alert, Peru does not have in place any informal trade control measures. INDECOPI is the reason for this status.

This reliance on the formalized INDECOPI process was challenged in 2011, when the National Service of Agricultural Sanitation (Servicio Nacional de Sanidad Agraria, or SENASA) established a mandatory phytosanitary certificate as a requirement for the entrance of certain textile products to Peruvian territory, through RM 28-2011-AG-SENASA-DSV. This measure, which could be regarded as a tariff-related measure and therefore an informal measure, was promptly criticized by several trade unions and academic organizations. The complaints mounted to such an extent that only two months later SENASA itself issued RM 34-2011-AG-SENASA-DSV revoking this requirement.

In contrast to Peru, Argentina adopted 65 informal measures during the same period, and China adopted 15 informal measures. Also, Indonesia adopted 12 such measures; the Russian Federation, 10; and India, 7.

The good example set by INDECOPI by its institutional character in Peru is also the result of the work done by former officials in other important government institutions, or by important public servants attracted to work for INDECOPI. Two significant examples are those of Fernando Zavala and Alfredo Ferrero. Fernando Zavala, general manager of INDECOPI from 1995 to 2000, later became vice minister and minister of economy and finance from 2002 to 2006. As discussed earlier, during his MEF years, Zavala focused on improving the practices of the ministry and promoted a very important ministry resolution, RM 005-2006-EF/15. It is evident that during the years that Zavala worked for INDECOPI, he developed a concern for expanding good practices in the agencies where he now has responsibilities. The second example is Alfredo Ferrero, former minister of commerce and tourism. After a long and successful career at MINCETUR (November 2003–July 2006), Ferrero joined INDECOPI's Council for the Defense of Competition.

Figure 2.7 Requests to Initiate Dumping, Subsidies, and Safeguards Investigations, 1992–2011

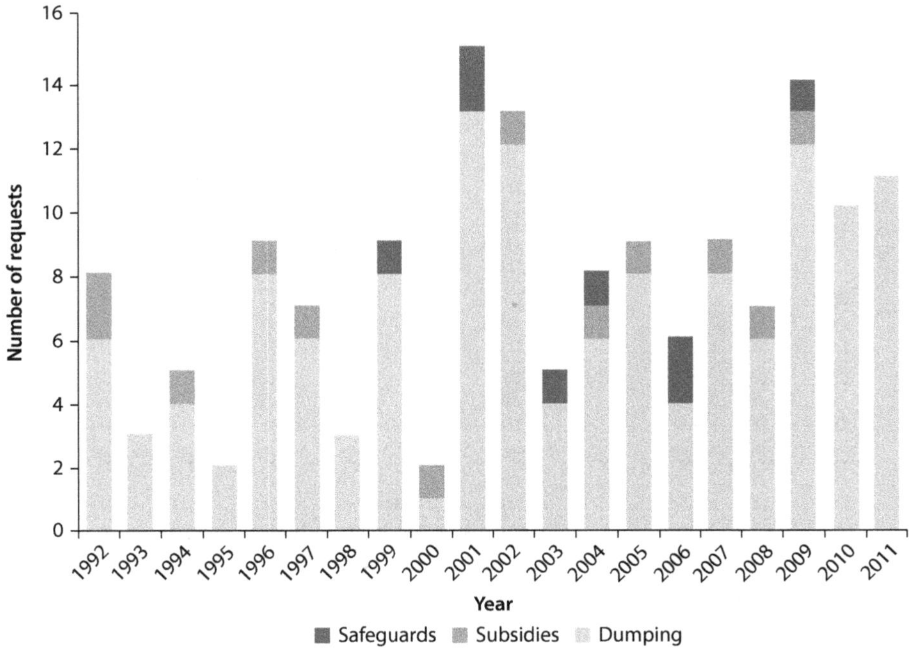

Source: Data from Dumping and Subsidies Control Office, National Institute for the Defense of Competition and the Protection of Intellectual Property.

With regard to INDECOPI's management of dumping and subsidies, between 2005 and 2011, the Dumping and Subsidies Control Committee received 66 requests to initiate dumping, subsidies, and safeguards investigations, as featured in figure 2.7. The number of requests represents an average of 9.4 requests per year between 2005 and 2011, compared with an average of 6.8 requests per year between 1992 and 2004.[14]

As figure 2.8 shows, of the 66 requests for 2005–11, only 45 had enough grounds to start an investigation, which means that only 68 percent of them were investigated. From 1992 to 2004, 68 investigations were initiated from a total of 89 requests, 76 percent of the requests. These data mean that from 2005 to 2011, 6.4 investigations were initiated per year, whereas from 1992 to 2004, only 5.2 investigations were initiated.

Apparently, both investigation requests and investigations initiated per year increased from 2005 to 2011 compared with the period from 1992 to 2004, but as we will see later, the significant increase in investigation requests and investigations initiated resulted from change-of-circumstances cases and sunset reviews cases. The latter are the continuation of the foregoing processes.

As figure 2.9 shows, 25 of the investigations from 2005 to 2011 concluded with definitive measures. This outcome means an average of 3.6 definitive

Figure 2.8 Dumping, Subsidies, and Safeguards Investigations Initiated, 1992–2011

Source: Data from Dumping and Subsidies Control Office, National Institute for the Defense of Competition and the Protection of Intellectual Property.

Figure 2.9 Dumping and Subsidies Investigations Resulting in Definitive Measures, 1992–2011

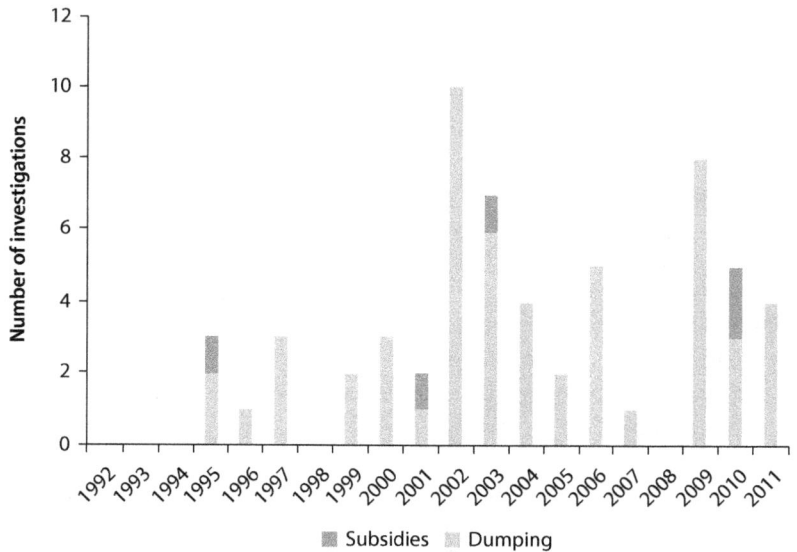

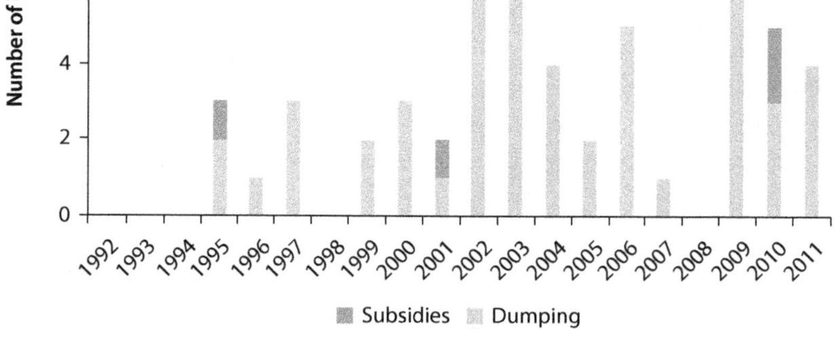

Source: Data from Dumping and Subsidies Control Office, National Institute for the Defense of Competition and the Protection of Intellectual Property.
Note: Over the period, no safeguards investigations resulted in definitive measures.

measures per year for this period compared with an average of 2.7 measures per year for the 1992–2004 period.

Note that in the first three years of the 1992–2004 period, no definitive measures were imposed. INDECOPI started working in 1993, and the first investigations were completed in 1995. Therefore, if we consider the 35 investigations that resulted in definitive measures in the 10-year period between 1995 and 2004, the average of measures imposed would be 3.5 per year, a figure similar to that for the period from 2005 to 2011.

Keeping in mind that 37 investigations were completed between 2005 and 2011 (figure 2.10), when comparing this figure with the number of cases that resulted in definitive measures in the same period (25), we conclude that definitive measures were imposed in 66 percent of the investigations.

If we analyze the origin of the 37 investigations completed between 2005 and 2011, we will see in figure 2.11 that only 35 percent of them are investigations of new claims. The remaining 65 percent correspond to investigations carried out because of sunset review or change of circumstances. It is important to highlight that the ex officio committee decided to initiate investigations because of change of circumstances in all old cases in which investigations had been conducted subject to legislation for non-WTO members. The cases were mainly for China, which became a WTO member during that period.

Tables 2.8 and 2.9 summarize the information on applications and measures taken both from 2005 to 2011 and from 1993 to 2004, broken down by type of

Figure 2.10 Number of Investigations Completed, 2005–11

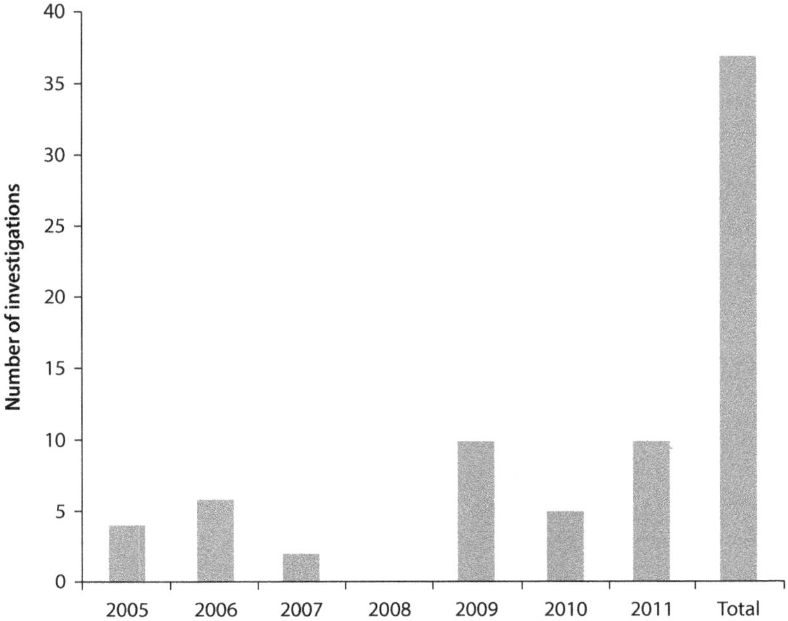

Source: Data from Dumping and Subsidies Control Office, National Institute for the Defense of Competition and the Protection of Intellectual Property.

Figure 2.11 Origin of Completed Investigations, 2005–11

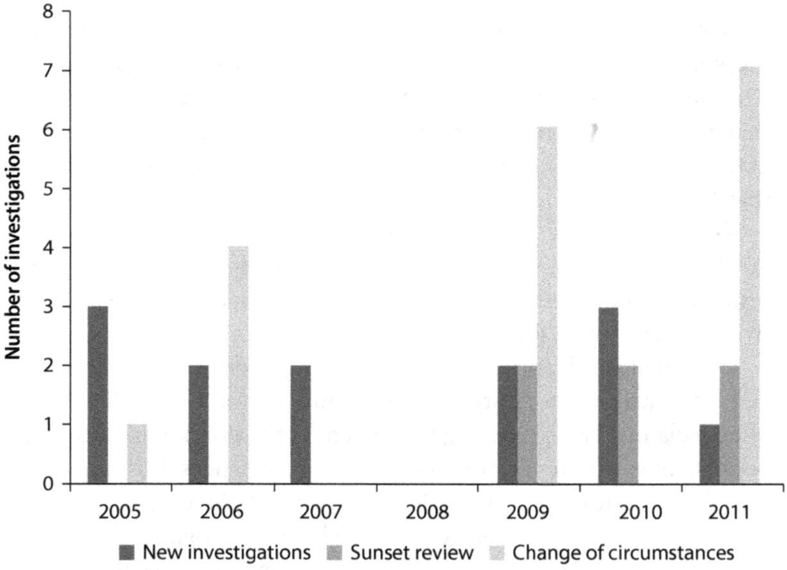

Source: Data from Dumping and Subsidies Control Office, National Institute for the Defense of Competition and the Protection of Intellectual Property.

Table 2.8 Numbers of Requests and Measures, 2005–11

	Total	*Subsidies*	*Safeguards*	*Dumping*
Requests	66	4	3	59
Investigations	45	3	1	41
Provisional right	6	1	0	5
Provisional and justified	0	0	0	0
Justified	25	2	0	23
Partly justified	5	0	0	5
Not justified	12	0	0	12
Pending resolution	0	0	0	0

Source: Data from Dumping and Subsidies Control Office, National Institute for the Defense of Competition and the Protection of Intellectual Property.

claim and by outcome. The relevance of dumping cases is significant compared with that of subsidies and safeguards. The latter dropped even more from 2005 to 2011.

Table 2.10 features the distribution of antidumping investigations broken down by economic sector. Investigations in the textile sector increased significantly compared with those in all sectors, but they include new investigations in the textile sector as well as changes in circumstances and sunset reviews.

Table 2.11 features investigations by economy. The economy with the highest number of claims against it in 2005–11 is China, followed by Kazakhstan; Russia; Brazil; Taiwan, China; and Argentina.

Table 2.9 Requests and Measures, 1993–2004

	Total	*Subsidies*	*Safeguards*	*Dumping*
Requests	81	7	4	70
Investigations	64	5	2	57
Provisional right	30	3	1	26
Provisional and justified	24	3	0	21
Justified	28	2	0	26
Partly justified	4	1	0	3
Not justified	28	2	1	25
Pending resolution	4	0	1	3

Source: Data from Dumping and Subsidies Control Office, National Institute for the Defense of Competition and the Protection of Intellectual Property. Table prepared by Raúl León and Carlos Carrillo.

Table 2.10 Antidumping Investigations by Sector, 1993–2011

Sector	*Total*	*1993–98*	*1999–2003*	*2005–11*
Agro-farming	8	2	4	2
Iron-steel	18	4	6	8
Tires	4	2	1	1
Textile	21	3	3	15
Meters	9	5	3	1
Footwear	6	1	2	3
Chemicals	6	2	3	1
Cement	2	0	0	2
Others	22	7	9	6
Total	96	26	31	39

Source: Data from Dumping and Subsidies Control Office, National Institute for the Defense of Competition and the Protection of Intellectual Property. Table prepared by Raúl León and Judith Vergara.

Central Reserve Bank of Peru

The BCRP is another example of a public institution with institutional management that not only allows it to attain its goals fully but also serves as an example to many other public institutions.

The board of directors of the BCRP comprises seven members. Four are appointed by the executive power. Congress ratifies those four members and appoints the remaining three.

The BCRP has maintained a technical profile throughout its history, since its foundation in 1922. For this purpose, the BCRP has been especially careful in creating a meritocratic organization that allows for adequate professional development of its officials and constantly attracts the best professionals from its sector and provides them with the best training so that they can better carry out their duties.

For instance, the current chair of the BCRP, Julio Velarde, who has been in office since September 2006, has told us that throughout his years of service within the BCRP, he has not had to fill the main leadership positions with any external officials. All the management teams have made their career in the BCRP.

Table 2.11 Antidumping Investigations by Economy, 1993–2011

	1993–2003				*2005–11*			
Economy	*Total*	*Dumping*	*Subsidies*	*Safeguards*	*Total*	*Dumping*	*Subsidies*	*Safeguards*
Argentina	9	7	2	0	2	2	0	0
Bolivia, Colombia, and Venezuela, RB	4	4	0	0	0	0	0	0
Brazil	6	5	1	0	3	3	0	0
Chile	11	11	0	0	1	1	0	0
China	20	19	0	1	11	11	0	0
Dominican Republic	0	0	0	0	1	1	0	0
Europe	2	1	1	0		0	0	0
France, Greece, Italy, Portugal, and Spain	0	0	0	0	1	0	1	0
India	0	0	0	0	1	1	0	0
Kazakhstan	0	0	0	0	5	5	0	0
Mexico	3	3	0	0	2	2	0	0
Pakistan	0	0	0	0	1	1	0	0
Romania	0	0	0	0	1	1	0	0
Russian Federation	0	0	0	0	5	5	0	0
Taiwan, China	0	0	0	0	3	3	0	0
Ukraine	0	0	0	0	1	1	0	0
United States	0	0	0	0	2	1	1	0
Vietnam	0	0	0	0	1	1	0	0
Nonmembers of the World Trade Organization	7	6	0	1	0	0	0	0
Other Asian economies	7	7	0	0	0	0	0	0
Others	2	1	1	0	0	0	0	0

Source: Data from Dumping and Subsidies Control Office, National Institute for the Defense of Competition and the Protection of Intellectual Property. Table prepared by Raúl León and Judith Vergara.

The general manager of the BCRP, Renato Rossini, told us that the BCRP's mandate is to control inflation by adjusting interest rates. The bank is not interested in helping specific sectors, such as exporters, but in safeguarding monetary stability.

The BCRP participates in the foreign currency exchange market, which is totally free in Peru. The BCRP works to prevent high short-term volatility in the exchange rate that may, for instance, affect the banking system, because a significant percentage of the total loans of the banking system are foreign currency loans. Short-term situations can occur, such as the sale of foreign currency by companies because of tax payments and speculation by local or foreign financing agents. The BCRP then reacts by selling or buying foreign currency in the market.

The exchange rate fluctuations of the foreign exchange operations by the BCRP are featured in figure 2.12. The figure shows how the BCRP, in buying and selling foreign currency, attempts to reduce short-term fluctuations but has no interest in affecting long-term trends.

In the eyes of the public, the position of board chair of the BCRP and the position of minister of economy and finance are fundamental for the development of the economy. Therefore, the appointment of these officials by

Figure 2.12 Exchange Operations vs. Exchange Rate, 1992–2012

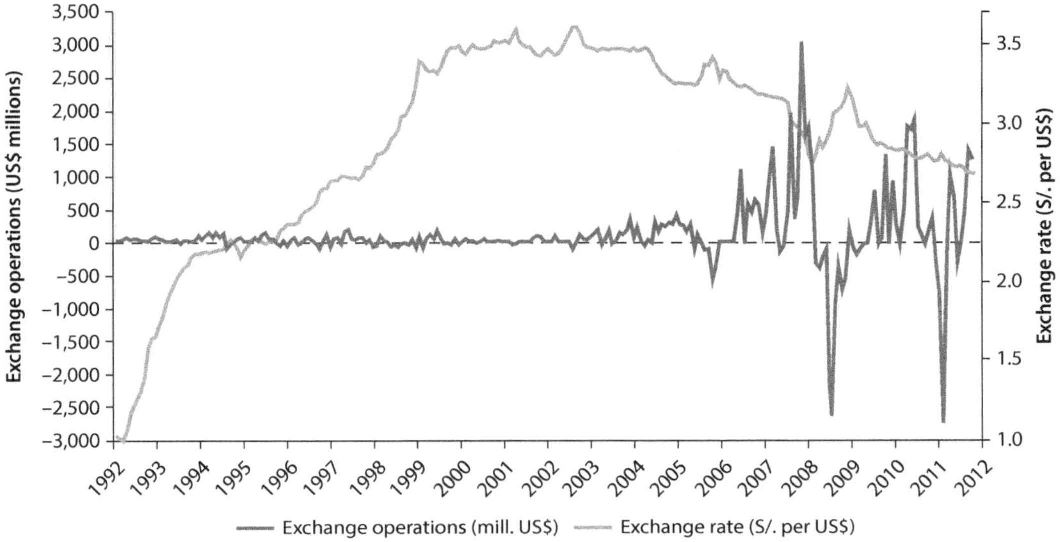

Source: Data from Central Reserve Bank of Peru. Figure prepared by Raúl León and Judith Vergara.

the president is an important indicator of what the president's economic policy will be. When new governments took office in 2001, 2006, and 2011, the presidents-elect had won without achieving a majority in the Congress. Hence, the public demanded to know, immediately after the results of the elections were revealed, not only whom the president-elect planned to appoint but also whether those individuals would be first-class officials. In all three cases, the appointments were almost unanimously applauded.

One of the darkest times for the BCRP occurred probably between 1985 and 1990, during the first administration of Alan García. During that period, because of the flawed economic policy of substituting imports, entrepreneurs had to go through a maze of administrative procedures to get their import licenses and foreign exchange use licenses approved. Nowadays, Argentina is going through a similar situation. The BCRP became involved in this procedure, which diverted it from its institutional goals and affected its technical management.

Maybe for this reason, the BCRP defines its vision as follows:

> We are acknowledged as an autonomous, modern, first-class Central Bank according to international standards, a role model in terms of our institutional character and high credibility in the country. We managed to regain the trust of the population in our national currency. Our staff is highly qualified, motivated, committed, and efficient and works in a collaborative environment where information and knowledge are shared.[15]

The sole mission of the BCRP is preserving the monetary stability. The BCRP's success in controlling the inflation rate confirms that the institution is properly managed by highly qualified professionals.

Final Remarks

Without disparaging the outstanding results that the economic reform provided in the 1990–2000 decade, we are pleased to point out that the economic results were even better in the 2001–10 decade. At the same time, governance in MEF and MINCETUR (together with the BCRP and INDECOPI, the most important and influential institutions of the economic reform) improved dramatically.

Dramatic improvement in governance in MEF and MINCETUR occurred under the democratic governments of the 2001–10 decade. Compared with authoritarian regimes, democratic regimes appear to be better able to attract the best professionals. The myth that only an authoritarian government will undertake economic reform is disproved by Peru's example. Democratic regimes not only rally the best but also allow reforms to continue until important goals are achieved. In contrast, continuity in authoritarian regimes is more related to relationships with the powerful.

Continuity based on performance and goals provides the government sector with experience and sophistication that allow it to achieve even the unimaginable. Great results are the product of great work. As we will emphasis in chapter 4, good economics is not a simple matter of finding the magic formula and then leaving things on automatic pilot. This thinking constitutes a second myth, one that is common in Peru but does not withstand scrutiny.

Trade reform has been one of the areas of economic policy where improvement in governance has taken hold, and the continuing challenge is to extend such attitudes and approaches to other government areas, such as education, health, and technology promotion. If this challenge can be met, Peruvian society can aspire to and achieve anything.

Annex 2A: Tariff Structure in Peru

	National subheadings		*Import value (cost, insurance, and freight), 2011*	
Ad valorem tariff rates (%)	*Number*	*Percent*	*US$ millions*	*Percent*
0	4,224	55.9	28,160.6	74.7
6	2,528	33.6	8,154.8	21.6
11	792	10.5	1,380.5	3.7
Total	7,554	100.0	37,695.9	100.0
Simple, nominal tariff				3.2
Tariff dispersion (standard deviation)				3.8
Effective tariff[a]				1.3
Weighted average tariff on imports				1.7

Source: Supervisory Agency for Customs and Tax Administration based on the customs tariff for 2012, as approved in Supreme Decree 238-211-EF, published 2011.

Note: Subheadings for chapter 98 of the customs tariff, "Goods with Special Treatment," are not included.

a. The effective rate is the amount of ad valorem tariff (cost, insurance, and freight) collected divided by the amount of tariff on imports (cost, insurance, and freight) multiplied by 100. Import data is for 2011.

Annex 2B: Tariff Structure by Type of Good

	Consumer goods		*Intermediate goods*		*Capital goods*		*Total*	
Ad valorem tariff rates (%)	*Number of subheadings*	*Cost, insurance, and freight value (US$ millions)*	*Number of subheadings*	*Cost, insurance, and freight value (US$ millions)*	*Number of subheadings*	*Cost, insurance, and freight value (US$ millions)*	*Number of subheadings*	*Cost, insurance, and freight value (US$ millions)*
0	465	1,163	2,113	14,578	1,646	12,419	4,224	28,161
6	1,097	4,760	1,441	3,394	0	0	2,538	8,155
11	419	922	373	458	0	0	792	1,381
Total	1,981	6,846	3,927	18,431	1,646	12,419	7,554	37,696
Percentage distribution								
0	23	17	54	79	100	100	56	75
6	55	70	37	18			34	22
11	21	13	9	2			10	2
Total	100	100	100	100	100	100	100	100
Average nominal tariff		5.6		3.2		0		3.2
Tariff dispersion		3.7		3.8		0		3.8

Source: Supervisory Agency for Customs and Tax Administration based on the customs tariff for 2012, as approved in Supreme Decree 238-211-EF.
Note: Sums may not total because of rounding. Subheadings for chapter 98 of the customs tariff, "Goods with Special Treatment," are not included.

Notes

1. Webb is director of the Instituto del Perú of the Universidad de San Martin de Porres.
2. The English-language website for the MMM, which contains the latest version of the document, is http://www.mef.gob.pe/index.php?option=com_content&view=article&id=2104&Itemid=101445&lang=en.
3. Finger, Ingco, and Reinecke (1996) provide comparisons between WTO bound rates and national legally imposed rates.
4. On its website, the Pacific Basin Economic Council describes itself as "a distinctly apolitical pro-business association bringing together business leaders across Asia Pacific." The council claims to be "actively engaged in promoting free trade and investment through open markets." See http://www.pbec.org/index.php?option=com_content&task=view&id=613&Itemid=1.
5. This effort was a real-world application of a point generalized by Mancur Olson (1971). Changing the track of policy often requires creation of a new institution; reorientation of an old one would be nearly impossible.
6. Five days later, DS 144-2002-EF was published. It was then clarified that DS 135-2002-EF applied only to *new* pieces of machinery and equipment.
7. The quotation is from an interview with Aráoz. In the course of the second, nonconsecutive administration of Alan García Pérez, Aráoz held the following positions: minister of foreign commerce and tourism, minister of production, and minister of economy and finance. Later on, she ran for president of the republic under Partido Aprista Peruano, the political party led by former president Alan García.
8. For more information, see MINCETUR's website on commercial agreements, http://www.acuerdoscomerciales.gob.pe.
9. The quotation is from an interview with Ferreyros.
10. The text of the agreement is available at http://www.ustr.gov/trade-agreements/free-trade-agreements/peru-tpa.
11. See the discussion of the Peru Trade Promotion Agreement at http://www.ustr.gov/trade-agreements/free-trade-agreements/peru-tpa.
12. For more information, see MINCETUR's website on commercial agreements, http://www.acuerdoscomerciales.gob.pe.
13. The quotations are from an interview with Thorne.
14. In early 1992, several cases were accepted by a provisional committee. As soon as INDECOPI began to function, it took over these cases.
15. The quotation is from BCRP's website at http://www.bcrp.gob.pe/sobre-el-bcrp/papel-del-bcrp.html.

References

Boloña, Carlos, and Javier Illescas. 1997. *Políticas arancelarias en el Perú, 1980–1997*. Lima: Free Market Economy Institute and San Ignacio de Loyola University.

Ferrero, Alfred. 2010. *Historia de un desafío: A la conquista de EE.UU. y el mundo* [Story of a Challenge: To the Conquest of the United States and the World]. Lima: Planeta.

Finger, J. Michael, Merlinda Ingco, and Ulrich Reinecke. 1996. *The Uruguay Round: Statistics on Tariff Concessions Given and Received*. Washington, DC: World Bank.

Finger, J. Michael, and Julio J. Nogués, eds. 2006. *Safeguards and Antidumping in Latin American Trade Liberalization: Fighting Fire with Fire*. New York: Palgrave Macmillan.

García Pérez, Alan. 2011. *Contra el temor económico: Creer en el Perú* [Against Economic Fear: Believing in Peru]. Lima: Planeta.

MEF (Ministry of Economy and Finance). 2003. *Multiannual Macroeconomic Framework 2003*. Lima: MEF. http://www.bcrp.gob.pe/docs/publicaciones/programa-economico/M-M-M-2004-2006-mayo-2003.pdf.

———. 2005. *Tariff Policy Guidelines*. Ministry Resolution 005-2006-EF/15. Lima: MEF. http://www.mef.gob.pe/contenidos/pol_econ/econ_internac/resoluciones/rm005-2006ef15.pdf.

———. 2006. *Guidebook for the Economic and Legal Analysis of Regulatory Production in MEF*. Ministry Resolution 639-2006-EF. Lima: MEF.

Olson, Mancur. 1971. *The Logic of Collective Action*. Cambridge, MA: Harvard University Press.

Webb, Richard, Diether Beuermann, and Carla Revilla. 2011. *La construcción del derecho de propiedad: El caso de los asentamientos humanos en el Perú*. Lima: Colegio de Notarios de Lima.

CHAPTER 3

Import Substitution under the World Trade Organization: Argentina

Introduction

During the past decade, two episodes have marked most countries' trade policies: (a) the rapid increase in world food prices and (b) the international recession that followed the Lehman Brothers debacle. Evidence shows that the measures implemented in response to rapidly rising food prices crucially depend on whether the country is a net importer or a net exporter. As an important net exporter, Argentina has increased its export barriers to a degree and scope unlikely surpassed by any other country.

The international recession also triggered increasing import barriers, usually, but not exclusively, through a greater reliance on nontariff measures, including contingent protection. Whereas the previous reforms had included the adoption of objective and procedurally transparent instruments—the trade remedies prescribed by the World Trade Organization (WTO)—as the principal instruments for managing trade restrictions, the new policies have in large part been decided and administered through other processes. These new policies amount to a significant reversal of the reforms of the 1990s—both in the extent of restrictions imposed and in the processes through which such policies are decided and administered.

The evidence to be presented indicates that WTO rules against such actions have not prevented the implementation of extensive import substitution measures. Dispute resolution pressures from other members have come with a long delay and until now have had no impact on Argentina's trade policies. As we concluded in *Safeguards and Antidumping in Latin American Trade Liberalization: Fighting Fire with Fire* (Finger and Nogués 2006), WTO rules provide support for governments that want to manage trade policies through transparent processes. We add here the further conclusion that these rules will not prevent a government set on doing so from introducing extensive import controls that amount to the reintroduction of an import substitution regime. Likewise, the Asunción Treaty, which includes the basic principle that goods will move freely within the member states of MERCOSUR (Mercado Común del Sur, or the Common Market of the South), has not prevented new restrictions on imports from within MERCOSUR.

The purpose of this chapter is to offer an illustration of the nature and extent of the trade policies implemented during the past decade. Toward this goal, the rest of the chapter is organized as follows. The next section offers a historical overview of the country's trade policies and the economic and social costs associated with its long-standing and extreme import substitution strategy. The third section contrasts the terms of trade and the behavior of the balance of payments over the reform decade with their behavior in the following decade in which the reforms were abandoned. The fourth section offers a detailed examination of the recent trend of import restriction and import substitution policies, including import licenses, antidumping, industrial promotion, and foreign exchange controls. The fifth section looks at other import substitution policies. The sixth section summarizes trends in export taxes and quantitative restrictions (QRs) on the export of agricultural products. It also looks at food subsidies that have had a significant effect on agricultural exports and analyzes some of the price effects of these measures. The seventh section addresses the international challenges faced by the country because of Argentina's restrictive measures; these challenges include unilateral retaliation as well as legal complaints under the WTO Dispute Settlement Understanding. The final section offers concluding remarks.

Import Substitution in Historical Perspective

Recently, President Cristina Fernández de Kirchner stated that her administration would like to push import substitution to a degree that would even ban imports of construction nails (Delletorre 2011). This policy stance again raises questions about the social and economic consequences of the country's long-standing import substitution policies. The chapter on Argentina in *Fighting Fire with Fire* (Nogués and Baracat 2006) covered the period from the late 1980s until about 2003, when trade liberalization through privatization and deregulation were implemented. Although Argentina had maintained a relatively open trade policy in the 19th century, a major shift toward an import substitution regime took place in the 1940s, when, during the presidencies of Juan Perón, imports of anything produced in the country were banned. Except for the period on which Nogués and Baracat (2006) focus, highly protectionist policies have been in place ever since.[1]

Looking at industrialization trends since the early 1940s and the country's failure to achieve efficiency in this and other sectors, Llach (2002) characterizes Argentina in the following way:

> This failure [referring to the failure to achieve an efficient industry] is not surprising because the 40 years witnessed, above all things, a dramatic deterioration of institutions. Only one constitutional president was left office, four civilian presidents were removed or overthrown, there were 10 successful coups, and so many failed that

> computing them challenges the neatness of the historian. In this context of nearly permanent illegality, ... violence was increasing and reached its pinnacle in the almost 15 years beginning after 1966 .... This was not all, because at the end of the period, Argentina was on the very brink of war with Chile and then ventured into a war against the United Kingdom after the occupation of the Malvinas Islands (author's translation).

Since the early 1980s, Argentina has followed two quite extreme sets of trade policies, both of which were put in place by freely elected governments. Elected in 1983 and pushed in part by pressures arising from the Latin American debt crisis, President Raúl Alfonsín overturned the ill-conceived trade liberalization program that his administration had inherited from the previous military regime.[2] Alfonsín later reversed himself on trade policy, and before he left office in 1989, his government was attempting to move toward an open economy. This effort was deepened by President Carlos Menem during the 1990s, and for a few years the country moved to an open economy strategy (Nogués and Baracat 2006).

As has occurred several times in Argentina since the 1940s, expansionary macroeconomic policies led once again to a severe overvaluation of the peso and a major devaluation. The collapse of convertibility (soon after the devaluation, what had been an exchange rate of Arg$1 to US$1 increased to more than Arg$4 to US$1) brought the economic crisis of 2001–02 and triggered political chaos. Eventually, in 2003, a new president was democratically elected. President Néstor Kirchner began the policy reversal from openness to an inward-looking strategy, and his successor, Cristina Fernández de Kirchner, has continued and extended this strategy.

Over the decades, Argentina's import substitution strategy has been extreme and can be described as import limits on any product produced within the country—and often too on any product that interest groups argued the country could produce (Nogués 2011b). The evidence to be provided in later sections leaves no room for doubt that Argentina has reversed its trade liberalization of the 1990s. As history has shown, although import barriers may provide a temporary stimulus, their application over the longer term carries considerable risk of retarding long-term growth.

Intellectually, import substitution is a major component of an economic philosophy that views domestic demand as the most significant engine of growth. The import substitution philosophy also presumes that major and pervasive errors exist in the signals that markets provide for resource allocation and that governments are capable of correcting those errors through direct intervention (subsidies, taxes, trade controls, and top-down orders) or public ownership.[3]

Finally, that philosophy overlooks the importance of the discipline that openness to international competition provides. History offers many examples of times when the domestic market has been exploited from a monopoly position and domestic producers—with reference to international norms—have become less and less productive.

Politics during the decade following the crisis that led to the resignation of Minister of Economy Domingo Cavallo, followed by that of President Fernando de la Rúa, in late 2001 attributed the social costs of the crisis following devaluation to high debt and open trade policies. These politics have made no attempt to disentangle the distinctive effects that overvaluation relative to open trade policies had on employment and tradable sectors generally, and this confusion in the public mind has facilitated the return of import substitution policies.

The Government's Current Perspective

Argentine authorities view the recently introduced restrictions as the only practical solution for preventing further deterioration of the current account balance in the short term. After the 2009 crisis, imports expanded by 45 percent in 2010 and 31 percent in 2011, whereas exports expanded by only 22 percent in 2010 and 24 percent in 2011. The trade balance surplus decreased from US$18.5 billion in 2010 to US$13.5 billion in 2011. In turn, the current account balance dropped from US$11 billion in 2010 to near zero in 2011. In addition, 2012 brought high interest payments and amortizations. With limited access to international financial markets, the government viewed such extreme measures as necessary to prevent further worsening of the external accounts. The shift of demand to domestically produced goods through import restrictions and the increase of demand from the government—government expenditures have grown from 31 percent of gross domestic product (GDP) in 2006 to about 42 percent in 2011—have produced a significant increase in gross national product.

An Extended Perspective

History indicates, however, that the country's return to inward-looking policies risks a return to the country's economic decline relative to countries with similar resource endowments that have maintained a more open trade strategy. These policies also contrast sharply with the open economy strategies implemented and sustained for the past two or three decades by neighboring countries such as Chile, Colombia, Mexico, and Peru. In the Latin American region, Argentina remains one of the very few countries characterized by quite extreme policies restricting imports.

The experiences of many countries indicate that, if sustained over the longer term, restrictions on imports and capital flows risk reducing the ability and willingness of the productive sector to invest, grow, and create jobs. Though it is still early to quantify the role of restrictive domestic policies in the current growth deceleration, most recent market data indicate that these policies have already had an impact on growth in some sectors. In particular, sectors such as construction and housing, which are heavily dollarized, have been going through a contraction as the medium of transaction—the U.S. dollar—has become scarce. Producers are also reporting shortages in inputs. Productive investment activities are being hurt as firms have difficulty in accessing foreign exchange to finance imported machinery. Similarly, opportunities for innovation and technology absorption are being hurt because of more restricted access to foreign technology and inputs.

On balance, international evidence suggests that even temporary trade barriers can have long-run costs. Substantial evidence from cross-country studies and case studies confirms the positive link between trade openness and growth.[4] Even when potential short-term benefits from import restrictions exist, they should be weighed against the possible negative consequences and international evidence on trade and growth. In particular, evidence indicates that South-South exports may not resume at the same level once temporary trade barriers are dismantled (Bown 2012). In the case of Argentina, examples of these effects span over several products, including wheat and bovine meat, where controls have implied significant reductions in output and export levels.

Long-Run Comparison with Australia

Argentina's prolonged experience with import substitution policies has come at very high social and economic costs. Its sustained long-run decline is striking when compared with the situation in countries such as Australia, which since the late 1940s has maintained a higher degree of openness than Argentina and over recent decades has come close to embracing free trade.[5] Figure 3.1 shows that in relation to Australia's per capita GDP, in the early 2000s Argentina was standing close to where it was in the 1870s. The inverted U shape indicates that Argentina nearly caught up with Australia during the early decades of the 20th century; however, the relative decline that started in the mid-1940s has continued unabated (Gerchunoff and Fajgelbaum 2005).

Figure 3.2 shows the long-run behavior of Argentina's and Australia's ratios of wages to GDP per worker. The peak for Argentina came in the mid-1940s when Perón used the foreign exchange resources that the country had accumulated during World War II to finance a historically high increase in real wages, estimated to have reached 48 percent between 1946 and 1948 (Llach 2002). After that

Figure 3.1 Ratio between Argentina's and Australia's per Capita GDP, 1870–2003

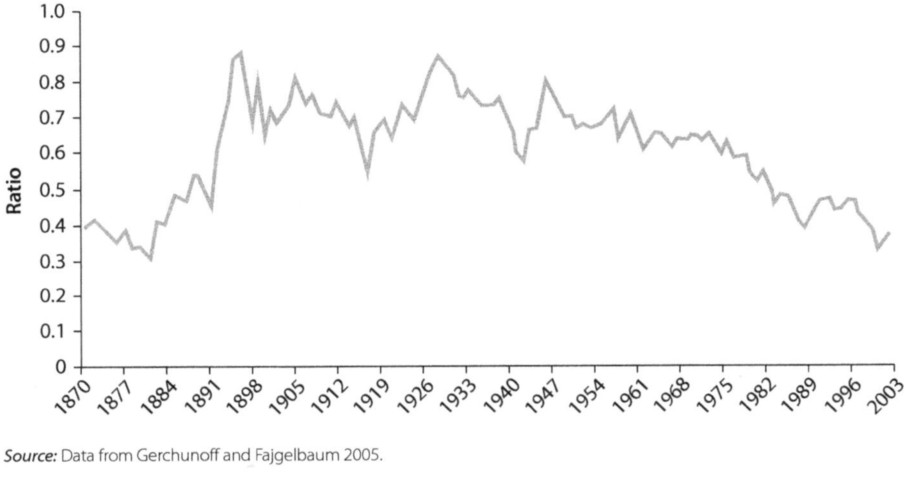

Source: Data from Gerchunoff and Fajgelbaum 2005.

Figure 3.2 Ratio of Wages to GDP per Worker: Argentina and Australia, 1901–2000

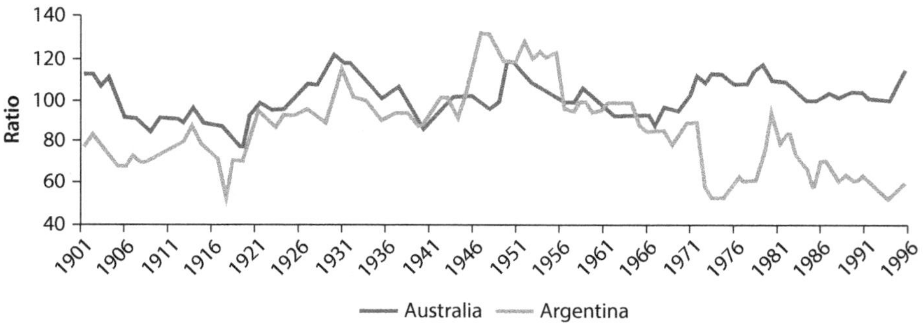

Source: Data from Gerchunoff and Fajgelbaum 2005.
Note: 1945 = 100.

episode, Argentina's share of wages in GDP per worker shows, in relation to Australia's, a sustained long-run decline.

The politics of protection in Argentina often refers to the creation of jobs and higher wages. The long-run behavior of this ratio (wages to GDP per worker) suggests, however, an economy where high protection has been accompanied by an income distribution process that in relative terms has deteriorated quite systematically with respect to workers (Nogués 2011b).

In sum, since the 1940s, Argentina has mostly embraced inward-looking policies and has experienced poor economic performance compared with economies that have accepted the discipline as well as the opportunities provided by integration into the international economy. From the perspective of institutional economics, trade restrictions are what Acemoglu and Robinson (2012) describe as "extractive political institutions."[6] Acemoglu and Robinson demonstrate that historically such institutions have stifled individual initiative and that economies in which they dominate have exhibited relatively poor economic performance—by standards of income distribution as well as of growth.

During most of this experience, Argentina was not bound by regional or multilateral obligations. But the signing of the Asunción Treaty that created MERCOSUR and of the Uruguay Round agreements in the mid-1990s changed this state of affairs. Nevertheless, as will be argued later, these new international obligations have not prevented Argentina from returning to its traditional import substitution policies.

The External Environment in Reform Years and Since

Following decades of relative stagnation, most of the 1990s were characterized by an important increase in trade dynamism. Table 3.1 shows that, starting from a low base, between 1990 and 1998 exports grew by 114 percent and imports grew by 670 percent (annex 3A offers brief comments on trade flows by origin or destination and type of goods). In a country that had remained closed and

Table 3.1 Trade, Terms of Trade, and the Multilateral Real Exchange Rate, Argentina, 1990–2010

Year	Imports (US$ millions)	Exports (US$ millions)	Trade balance (US$ millions)	Multilateral real exchange rate (%)		Current account (US$ millions)	Terms of trade index (1990 = 100)
				(1)	(2)		
1990	4,077	12,353	8,276	n.a.	n.a.	n.a.	100
1991	8,275	11,978	−3,703	100	n.a.	n.a.	101
1992	14,872	12,235	−2,637	125	n.a.	−5,558	108
1993	16,784	13,118	−3,666	113	n.a.	−8,209	111
1994	20,077	15,839	−4,238	113	n.a.	−10,981	112
1995	20,122	20,963	841	113	n.a.	−5,104	112
1996	23,762	23,811	49	122	n.a.	−6,755	121
1997	30,450	26,431	−4,019	117	n.a.	−12,116	120
1998	31,377	26,434	−4,943	113	n.a.	−14,465	113
1999	25,508	23,309	−2,199	103	n.a.	−11,910	107
2000	25,280	26,341	−1,061	104	n.a.	−8,955	118
2001	20,321	26,543	6,222	99	n.a.	−3,780	117
2002	8,990	25,651	16,661	236	n.a.	8,767	116
2003	13,833	29,939	16,106	216	n.a.	8,140	127
2004	22,445	34,576	12,131	225	n.a.	3,212	129
2005	28,687	40,387	11,700	230	n.a.	5,274	126
2006	34,151	46,546	12,395	236	n.a.	7,768	134
2007	44,707	55,980	11,273	243	237	7,354	140
2008	57,422	70,019	12,597	251	218	6,755	156
2009	38,780	55,672	16,892	270	209	11,062	156
2010	57,462	68,134	10,672	278	199	3,081	156

Sources: Except for the real exchange rate, data from National Institute of Statistics and Censuses (Instituto Nacional de Estadística y Censos, or INDEC). Data in the first column of real exchange rates are from the Central Bank of Argentina, and second column data are provided by the Institute for Economic Research on Argentina and Latin America.
Note: n.a. = not applicable.

underinvested for decades, import demand—particularly of capital goods—grew fast, and the resulting trade and current account deficits were financed with capital inflows, including foreign direct investment. During those years, the country attracted capital, but at the same time, the peso became increasingly overvalued—the cycle continued.[7]

Moreover, world markets for the products Argentina exports have been favorable. Table 3.2 shows that world imports of the goods and services exported by Argentina increased by 11.0 percent per year over the 2001–11 decade, compared with 10.4 percent per year for the export bundle of Peru and 10.0 percent per year for all world imports.

The swing from consecutive current account deficits during the 1990s to consecutive surpluses during the 2000s allowed the government during the latter decade to disconnect the economy from international capital flows. Argentina repaid its debt to the International Monetary Fund in full, but the government has continued to borrow from República Bolivariana de Venezuela at high

Table 3.2 Comparison of the Growth of World Markets for Products Exported by Argentina and Peru, 2001–11

Exporting economy	*Rate of growth (%)*
Goods and services	
Argentina	11.0
Peru	10.4
World	10.0
Goods only	
Argentina	11.2
Peru	10.4
World	10.0

Sources: For trade data, the United Nations Commodity Trade Statistics Database (UN Comtrade); for service data, the World Bank's World Development Indicators Database.
Note: Annual growth rates of world imports by Standard International Trade Classification–1 categories were averaged using Argentina's and Peru's 2001 export composition as shares.

interest rates and from the World Bank and the Inter-American Development Bank, though not from private market sources. The absence of transparent and stable rules, an unreliable legal system, a complicit Congress, and a discretionary government have raised Argentina's level of country risk to one of the top positions in the world. Slowly but surely, since late 2011, the need for foreign exchange reappeared, the trade surplus narrowed, and capital flight accelerated.[8] This trend is the consequence of a domestic currency that, with a quasi-fixed exchange rate and inflation currently running at over 25 percent per year, has appreciated quickly.[9]

Among Latin American countries, Argentina has been characterized as having one of the most unstable and acute economic cycles (see Perry 2003 and the references therein). Over the past 80 years, the economy has gone through several cycles of devaluation followed by lax monetary and fiscal policies that bring renewed inflation. Targeting the exchange rate primarily at the control of inflation rather than at maintenance of parity between price levels inside and outside the country has often allowed overvaluation of the exchange rate. Overvaluation, in turn, has brought an increase in imports and the application of import restrictions. At some point, the overvalued exchange rate cannot be sustained and will bring another emergency devaluation.

The result, as Nogués (2011b) documents, is long-run economic performance that compares poorly with other countries with similar (and poorer) resource endowments. The cyclic resort to emergency and ad hoc restrictions means that more stable and transparent governance institutions that are evolving in other countries have not become a part of Argentina's governance profile.

Since 2011, overvaluation has deepened, not only as a consequence of the underlying domestic inflation but also because of the recent devaluation of Brazil's real exchange rate as well as the reduction in the price of Argentina's exportables associated with an uncertain international economy. In the process, foreign exchange reserves have declined in Argentina, and as in many past episodes, the government has responded by tightening exchange controls. This move has, in turn, triggered the reappearance of a parallel (black) market for foreign exchange that in early 2013 was trading at 70 percent above the official rate. This outcome again is part of the cycle through which the Argentine economy has passed several times.

If good times are appropriate for the institutionalization of governance reforms, then we can conclude that during the past decade Argentina lost an opportunity to consolidate the fundamentals that would have put the economy on a stronger and more sustainable long-run growth path. Not surprisingly, Argentina's current ranking in international comparative indexes, such as those reflecting government effectiveness, corruption, and rule of law, has deteriorated markedly, as illustrated by Bolsa de Comercio de Córdoba (2010). The discussion of the protectionist measures implemented during the previous decade demonstrates not only the extent of such measures but also the abandonment of the formalized processes that were part of previous reforms.

Trends in Import Barriers

In the introduction, we mentioned that to an important extent, import substitution measures are being implemented through quite discretionary processes. Table 3.3, from Global Trade Alert data, indicates that the bulk of measures implemented by Argentina between 2008 and 2011 can be classified as nontariff barriers.

As to process, the first four columns can be classified as measures implemented through relatively discretionary processes—in contrast to trade defense measures that according to WTO regulations must follow transparent and objective decision processes. The contrast with other Latin American countries regarding the number of measures implemented is striking. Also Argentina's share of measures put in place through less transparent processes reaches 49 percent, whereas the corresponding numbers are 13 percent for Brazil and 0 percent for Peru and Uruguay. The other side of the coin indicates that the share of Argentina's relatively WTO-transparent measures, like antidumping and safeguards, is low: 23 percent versus 63 percent for Brazil and 100 percent for Peru.

The following sections elaborate on the instruments that recent governments have used to reintroduce an import substitution strategy. The list includes import licenses, antidumping measures, regional fiscal incentives, and—more recently—severe foreign exchange controls.

Import Licenses

An import license is a requirement that is additional to those that must normally be met to satisfy customs formalities. In Argentina, license petitions were, until recently, administered by the Ministry of Industry. In a quite unexpected decision in December 2011, shortly after being sworn into power, the reelected president created the Secretariat of Foreign Trade under the Ministry of Economy. The new office is responsible for administering trade policies as well as overseeing trade negotiations. In practice, this structure implies a higher degree of centralization

Table 3.3 Formal and Informal Trade Restrictions Imposed by Economies, 2008–11

Economy	*Nontariff barrier (not otherwise specified)*	*Technical plus sanitary and phytosanitary measures*	*Bailout or state aid*	*Tariff measures plus import quotas plus import bans*	*Trade defense measure (antidumping, countervailing duty, safeguard)*	*Export taxes or restriction*	*Total of measures specified*	*Total of all measures tabulated by Global Trade Alert*
Russian Federation	1	4	41	48	15	13	122	156
Argentina	61	1	9	9	37	7	124	127
China	5	2	1	12	27	10	57	89
India	3	0	0	16	31	10	60	80
Brazil	3	0	1	24	19	1	48	63
European Union	0	0	1	3	29	1	34	38
Indonesia	6	3	3	8	3	5	28	37
United States	1	1	6	5	10	0	23	34
Korea, Rep.	0	0	5	5	0	0	10	26
South Africa	0	1	3	13	6	0	23	25
Ukraine	2	2	1	1	4	2	12	17
Vietnam	0	0	0	8	0	3	11	15
Malaysia	1	0	0	3	0	1	5	14
Turkey	0	0	0	4	7	0	11	12
Thailand	2	0	0	1	2	1	6	11
Egypt, Arab Rep.	0	0	1	2	1	3	7	9
Kenya	2	0	0	2	0	2	6	8

table continues next page

Table 3.3 Formal and Informal Trade Restrictions Imposed by Economies, 2008–11 *(continued)*

Economy	*Nontariff barrier (not otherwise specified)*	*Technical plus sanitary and phytosanitary measures*	*Bailout or state aid*	*Tariff measures plus import quotas plus import bans*	*Trade defense measure (antidumping, countervailing duty, safeguard)*	*Export taxes or restriction*	*Total of measures specified*	*Total of all measures tabulated by Global Trade Alert*
Peru	0	0	0	0	7	0	7	7
Switzerland	0	0	1	0	0	0	1	6
New Zealand	0	0	2	0	2	0	4	5
Zambia	0	0	0	3	0	1	4	5
Colombia	0	0	0	1	2	1	4	4
Ecuador	0	0	0	2	0	0	2	4
Philippines	0	0	0	2	1	0	3	4
Zimbabwe	0	1	0	2	0	1	4	4
Sri Lanka	0	0	0	2	0	0	2	3
Uganda	2	0	0	1	0	0	3	3
Chile	0	0	0	0	1	0	1	1
Costa Rica	0	0	0	0	0	0	0	1
El Salvador	0	0	0	0	0	0	0	0
Uruguay	0	0	0	0	0	0	0	0

Source: Based on Global Trade Alert data, "Implementing Country and Measure Type" (http://www.globaltradealert.org/data-exports).
Note: Countries are ranked by the total number of measures.

and trade control, because before the decision was implemented, trade policies were administered by the Ministry of Industry, whereas trade negotiations were the responsibility of the Foreign Affairs Ministry.[10]

Within the General Agreement on Tariffs and Trade (GATT)/WTO system, import licenses are allowed as instruments for administering restrictions that are permissible by some other GATT/WTO criterion. The allowance for import licensing is not intended to be a way to legalize whatever restriction such licenses administer.

WTO regulates two types of import licenses: automatic and nonautomatic. According to multilateral rules, following presentation of a license petition by an importer, automatic licenses must be decided within 10 days, whereas nonautomatic licenses (NALs) must normally be decided within 30 days but no more than 60 days. Furthermore, the WTO Agreement on Import Licensing Procedures[11] requires that these instruments be used with caution and satisfy several principles, including the following:

- They must not violate other WTO principles and obligations.
- They must be implemented in a transparent and predictable manner.
- The additional administrative burden to importers should be minimal.
- They must contain a consultative mechanism that offers solutions to differences that could arise in the administration of import licenses.

Automatic Licenses

Automatic import licenses were first applied in early 1999, shortly after the devaluation of the Brazilian real (Resolution 17/1999). At the time, the government considered that following the decline in world demand, imports of some sensitive products should be monitored. Events that slowed world growth included several crises, such as the Tequila crisis in 1994–95, the East Asian crisis in 1997, the Russian crisis in 1998, and the devaluation of the Brazilian real in 1999.[12] These crises put Argentina into a negative growth path that would last until 2003 (table 3.4). As a consequence by 2000, only a year after automatic import licenses had been implemented, the number of tariff lines covered by this instrument had increased to 560. And by 2005, when GDP growth was again well under way, the coverage had reached 1,546 tariff lines. Table 3.4 shows that by 2008 the number had increased to 1,551 tariff lines. These data indicate that during the past decade, the number of tariff lines covered by automatic licenses increased rapidly despite the massive 2002 devaluation, which until recently provided a high level of protection. The government has sometimes justified the use of automatic licenses as being necessary for checking compliance with technical standards. These justifications will be taken up later in the review of the WTO Committee on Import Licensing's discussion of Argentina's import licenses.

Most of the leverage the government has applied to importers to substitute domestic products or to arrange offsetting countertrade has been applied through NALs. Therefore, we now turn attention to this instrument.

Table 3.4 Legal Norms Adding or Subtracting Tariff Lines to the List of Automatic Licenses

Legal norm	*Number of tariff lines*	*Accumulated tariff lines*
Disposition 75/2000 by the undersecretary of industry	560	560
Disposition 2/2002	57	617
Disposition 9/2003	922[a]	922
Disposition 14/2003	41	963
Disposition 7/2004	8	971
Disposition 14/2004	−2	969
Disposition 26/2004	1	970
Disposition 8/2005	2	972
Disposition 9/2005	6	978
Disposition 15/2005	568	1,546
Decree 509/2007	1,532[a]	1,532
Disposition 8/2007	3	1,535
Disposition 10/2008	3	1,538
Disposition 11/2008	13	1,551

Source: Resolutions from Ministry of Industry.
a. Some dispositions add as well as delete products from the list.

Table 3.5 Import Coverage of Nonautomatic Licenses

Variable	*2010 Estimate*
Imports under nonautomatic licenses	US$11.990 billion
Total imports	US$56.501 billion
Import share	21.2%

Source: Estimates provided by Francis Ng, World Bank.

Nonautomatic Import Licenses

NALs[13] such as those used by Argentina can be categorized as a type of nontariff barrier. The recent experience is a salient example of how this instrument can be used to foster import substitution quite extensively. Table 3.5 shows that the 2010 import coverage of NALs in Argentina amounted to nearly US$12 billion, or 21 percent of total imports. As will also be seen, NALs have become a source of frustration for other WTO members.

Table 3.6 shows the products that are currently covered by NALs, as well as the corresponding ministerial resolutions. The protected products can generally be classified as produced by sensitive or declining sectors and include bicycles, motorcycles, housewares, toys, footwear, textiles, metals, tires, and automobiles.[14]

Also, in the WTO Committee on Import Licensing, the delegate from the European Union (EU) stated that 16 percent of Argentina's imports from this origin were covered by NALs (WTO 2011).[15]

In what follows, we discuss (a) the statistics and regulations or resolutions, (b) the transparency of the administrative process, (c) and the use of NALs as a means to foster import substitution. We also summarize the discussions held by the WTO Committee on Import Licensing.

Table 3.6 List of Products Requiring Nonautomatic Licenses

Product	*Ministerial resolution*	*Number of tariff lines, May 2011*
Paper and paperboard	Resolution 798/1999	4
Bicycles	Resolution 220/2003	62
Housewares[a]	Resolution 444/2004 Resolution 181/2008 Resolution 329/2008 Resolution 123/2009 Resolution 251/2009 Resolution 61/2009 Resolution 45/2011	23
Toys	Resolution 485/2005	20
Bicycle tires	Resolution 153/2005	14
Footwear[a]	Resolution 486/2005	29
Balls	Resolution 217/2007	1
Footwear parts[a]	Resolution 61/2007	1
Motorcycles	Resolution 689/2006 Resolution 195/2007 Resolution 45/2011	7
Textiles[a]	Resolution 343/2007 Resolution 330/2008 Resolution 13/2009 Resolution 251/2009 Resolution 61/2009 Resolution 123/2009	118
Metal products[a]	Resolution 588/2008 Resolution 251/2009 Resolution 61/2009 Resolution 45/2011	41
Knitted fabrics[a]	Resolution 589/2008 Resolution 13/2009 Resolution 251/2009 Resolution 45/2011	111
Other manufactured products	Resolution 47/2007 Resolution 13/2009 Resolution 61/2009 Resolution 251/2009 Resolution 45/2011	164
Tires[a]	Resolution 26/2009	5
Screws and volts	Resolution 165/2009 Resolution 45/2011	4
Auto parts	Resolution 337/2009 Resolution 45/2011	51
Automobiles	Resolution 45/2011	4
Total		659

Source: Based on legislation published at http://www.infoleg.com.ar.
a. Products listed in Moore (2011, table 9.2) for which antidumping investigations have been initiated in recent years.

Statistics and Ministerial Regulations or Resolutions. Resolution 798/1999 implemented the first NALs for the imports of some paper and paperboard products. At the time, the official justification was the need to ensure that imports complied with technical regulations. However, no significant change had occurred in the nature of the products being imported nor in their volume, and there was no explanation that the capacities that customs authorities applied to this verification in the past had been inadequate. In the review by the WTO Committee on Import Licensing, which is discussed further later, the committee found that the Argentine government cited the application of technical measures without documenting the need for such measures or their consistency with relevant WTO rules.

Table 3.6 shows a growing trend of tariff lines under NALs with two clear jumps. The first, in 2008–09, was probably triggered by the international crisis: the coverage of NALs increased from 158 tariff lines in 2007 to 479 in 2009–10. The second jump took place during the first half of 2011 when the economy was growing fast. Therefore, as has been the case with automatic licenses, NALs have been implemented during periods of fast growth and slow growth.

Considerable evidence, including several documents released by the government, demonstrates that the major goal of NALs is not compliance with technical regulations but achievement of import substitution targets. Resolution 444/2004 states that a certain harmony should exist between NALs and the objective of "stimulating national production" (authors' translation). Similarly, Resolution 689/2006 states that "in some types of motorcycles, there has been an important change in imports that requires monitoring" (authors' translation). However, the significant change in the importation of motorcycles had been the one caused by a policy change: a shift from the importation of finished articles to knock-down kits.

In no case has the government published the results of a contestable analysis, such as the WTO requirement for an antidumping measure. The WTO transparency and procedural requirements for NALs are significantly lower than those for contingent protection measures.

Administrative Uncertainty. There is evidence of delays in the approval of NALs that go well beyond the WTO-stipulated maximum of 60 days. Interviews with observers indicate that in some cases the government has taken more than 200 days. And as we will later describe, some members of the WTO Committee on Import Licensing have complained about exporters waiting 120 days—that is, double what the agreement requires. Members have questioned the legality under the import licensing agreement of the nontransparent and discretionary procedures through which they have applied. They have also questioned the use of NALs as an import restriction in and of itself.[16] The World Bank (2010) has also documented that in Argentina it takes on average 77 days for approval of a license application, well above the average for Latin America (46 days) and the world (30 days).

Forced Import Substitution and Countertrade Requirements. Administrative discretion has also been used to demand that approval of a NAL—and therefore the authorization to use a certain amount of foreign exchange for the approved imports—be compensated either with investment for domestic production (import substitution) or with exports. Essentially, the government's goal is to preserve current account neutrality for each importing business and in this way help the Central Bank to preserve its foreign exchange reserves.

These pressures that government places on business occur in a legal vacuum: no ministerial regulation indicates when and how the discretion to process a NAL should be used. According to our interviews, pressures have also been applied verbally and through other administrative procedures that leave no paper trail.

Many examples exist of NALs being used to force import substitution targets. For one, newspaper articles have announced an agreement between John Deere and the government according to which this firm would initiate production of harvesters in exchange for approval of NALs (Bertello 2011). Among other concepts, this article states, "Like other foreign-owned companies, because of NALs, John Deere has also in recent months faced serious obstacles to the import of finished products. The presumption is that as a consequence of the agreement with the government, this situation will begin to change" (authors' translation).

Here are some other examples taken from news articles and press releases issued by the Ministry of Industry:

- *Motorcycles.* At the opening of ExpoMoto, the minister of industry announced that in relation to the recession of 2009, motorcycle imports during 2010 declined by 200,000 units (Esteban 2011). Import substitution policy aided by NALs has convinced leading firms such as Honda, Yamaha, and Suzuki to invest and produce domestically. Furthermore, according to the official (government-supplied) information,
  - The Ministry of Industry now requires that for each imported motorcycle, two should be locally produced. This requirement will increase to four in 2012.
  - Importers that decide not to produce domestically are required to reduce imports by 40 percent, whereas producers of parts should reduce imports by 20 percent.
  - Finally, as a criticism of the 1990s and as a vindication of what the new policies will produce, the government-supplied information concludes, "This is a significant change in relation to the 1990s, when production declined from 100,000 units in 1993 to 26,000 in 2001."
- *Textiles.* At the 2011 Annual Convention of the Textile Agroindustry, the minister of industry asserted, among other things, the following (Ministry of Industry 2011b):
  - The ministry has worked to meet the objective of stopping imports.
  - Nonautomatic import licenses now cover 116 tariff lines, and nine antidumping investigations have been opened.

- Import substitution will reindustrialize Argentina through international firms, including Lacoste, Nike, Adidas, Puma, Levi Strauss, Wrangler, and Zara, as well as several Brazilian firms.
- In eight years, the textile sector has grown by 146 percent and created 500,000 new jobs. This progress contrasts with the situation in the 1990s, when the sector lost 180,000 jobs and 2,500 firms shut down.

- *Automobiles.* Several agreements between car companies and the government target import substitution and export objectives in exchange for being allowed to import luxury cars (Ministry of Industry 2011a, 2011c):
  - Wine and olive oil companies reached an agreement to export their products in exchange for being allowed to import Porsche cars of a similar value.
  - BMW agreed to balance its trade deficit through exports of several products, including exportables such as processed rice.
  - To close its trade deficit, Hyundai agreed to export soybean oil, biodiesel, and wine to Vietnam.
  - To receive permission to import cars and trucks, Fiat agreed to produce additional agricultural machinery that required an investment of about US$100 million.
  - Ford, Mercedes Benz, Alfa Romeo, Volkswagen, General Motors, Peugeot, and Citroën have agreed to balance their trade flows through different mixes of import substitution and exports.

  In a show of successful achievements made possible by these forced countertrade agreements, the ministers of industry and of economy announced in May 2011 that by 2012 the trade deficit of the auto sector would decline by US$4 billion (Ministry of Industry 2011c). The counting of products such as rice, wine, and olive oil as exports of the auto sector does not imply a change in the overall level of exports. These products are commodities and would likely have been sold in international markets without the efforts of the auto industry. Moreover, forcing car companies to export goods when they lack comparative advantage in the marketing of these products is likely to increase costs.
- *Other products.* Exports and investment for import substitution have been agreed to by other companies, including Blackberry and Samsung, which assemble knock-down kits in the Province of Tierra del Fuego.

WTO Discipline: Arguments and Criticisms about Argentina's NALs in the WTO Committee on Import Licensing

Discussions in the WTO Committee on Import Licensing regarding the administration of NALs by Argentina have been growing and becoming more severe. By 2010, some of Argentina's trading partners had registered several criticisms (table 3.7). In general, the intervening parties that are listed have endorsed what others have presented, so in this sense, at least the six countries in the table agree with all of the parties. Nevertheless, in the table, we attempt to signal the issues that each of the parties initially raised individually.

Table 3.7 Criticisms Raised by Argentina's Partners in the World Trade Organization Committee on Import Licensing until 2010

Type of criticism	*China*	*European Union*	*Japan*	*Mexico*[a]	*Peru*	*United States*
Delays	X	X	X			X
Administrative requirements	X	X			X	
Nondecisions or lack of transparency	X					X
Volatility					X	
Sensitivity					X	
Trade or investment compensation		X				X
Balance of payment						X
De facto import prohibition			X			X
Increased product coverage	X					X
Control of technical regulations		X				
Transitory nature		X			X	

Source: Based on World Trade Organization minutes of the meetings of the Committee on Import Licensing. The minutes are available at http://www.wto.org/spanish/tratop_s/implic_s/implic_s.htm.
a. Mexico simply endorsed the criticisms that other countries had previously mentioned.

Questions regarding delays in the approval process were first raised by the United States in 2004 for footwear and in 2007 for toys. Lack of a satisfactory response led the United States to repeat those questions in 2008 and later when, according to some of its exporters, the time for approval of NALs had increased to approximately 120 days. Other WTO members have also raised this issue.

In the committee meeting held in October 2009, Peru questioned Argentina's assertion that NALs were being used to protect sensitive sectors against international trade volatility. It also called attention to the increasing administrative information being requested for processing petitions. Also at this meeting, the United States extended its criticism of the requirement that trade compensation objectives be exchanged for approval of NALs. It argued that this requirement transformed the nature of the country's NAL regime into a QR for balance of payments purposes, and it requested that Argentina explain this policy.

The EU has also explicitly criticized the delays in approval, as well as raising the argument that NALs are used to verify compliance with Argentina's technical regulations.

At the April 2010 committee meeting, the United States argued that Argentina's management of import licenses represented a de facto prohibition against imports of several products and that discretion varied depending on the importing firm, the exporting country, and the product involved. It added that the evidence and lack of satisfactory response to several questions that members have raised since 2004 created doubts about Argentina's commitment to the principles of the 1994 GATT.

At the April 2010 meeting, the EU also argued that Argentina's measures were inflicting costs on several European exporters and requested a response before the EU would raise the matter in other WTO forums. Peru and the EU criticized Argentina's response that NALs were a transitory regime.

They pointed out that the system of NALs had been in place for several years, during which the product coverage continued to increase. Moreover, they pointed out that the term *transitory regime* had no meaning in the WTO except with respect to the specific limits the WTO agreement imposed on certain applications of licenses.

Japan added that its distance from Argentina and the 30-day limit provided in NALs on land products implied a de facto import prohibition from this origin. In article 3.5(g), the Agreement on Import Licensing states, "The period of license validity shall be of reasonable duration and ... shall not preclude imports from distant sources."

Argentina has responded to some of these questions. For example, it has stated that (a) the facts are different from those advanced by the complaining parties, (b) responses to NAL petitions have always been within the time limits established by the WTO agreement, and (c) changing conditions of international trade justify the licensing requirements and the length of time they have been in place. Argentina has not provided details as to what these "changing conditions" are, nor has it explained why more attention to compliance with standards is the appropriate response.

On March 30, 2012, several developing and developed economies signed a joint statement released by the WTO Council on Trade in Goods that reflects several of the frustrations that members had been raising at the WTO Committee on Import Licensing (see annex 3C for the text of the statement):

- The nonautomatic licensing requirement must comply with all relevant provisions of the Agreement on Import Licensing Procedures, including a maximum processing period of 60 days.
- Many companies have reported receiving telephone calls from Argentine government officials in which they are informed that they must agree to undertake such trade-balancing commitments before receiving authorization to import goods.
- The committee was not aware of any official directive or resolution setting out these trade-balancing or investment requirements.
- Argentina should provide a detailed written explanation of why in its view these measures and practices are consistent with WTO rules.

The third point is particularly worrisome because it indicates that import barriers are being implemented in a legal vacuum that leaves ample room for discretion.

The following conclusions emerge from the discussions at the WTO Committee on Import Licensing and the Council on Trade in Goods:

- Developing and industrial countries alike have actively criticized the administration of the country's NAL regime and have questioned its consistency with WTO obligations.
- These members have found Argentina's responses unsatisfactory.

- No MERCOSUR members have actively participated in the committee's discussions.
- Thus far, pressures and criticisms have not pushed the country to move closer to the principles of its WTO obligations.[17]

The complete WTO statement, which is provided in annex 3C, reflects WTO members' high degree of frustration with Argentina's policies.

Antidumping

Since 2001, Argentina has conducted no countervailing measure investigation and only one safeguard investigation. That investigation reached an affirmative determination and resulted in additional tariffs being imposed in 2007 on imports of recordable compact discs for a period of three years. Imports came principally from China. As with most other WTO members, Argentina has used antidumping much more frequently than safeguards or countervailing measures.

The next section covers the following points: (a) the changing links between trade policy institutions and the antidumping mechanism, (b) administrative adjustments and outcomes of the antidumping investigations, (c) antidumping measures by target countries, and (d) trade coverage of antidumping measures.

Trade Policy Institutions and the Antidumping Mechanism

Latin American leaders of the 1990s, foreseeing that protectionist governments would eventually reappear, attempted to place obstacles against a possible reimplementation of import substitution policies. In the case of Argentina, these measures included binding the maximum tariff rate in the WTO at 35 percent and adopting the MERCOSUR common external tariff. Under the country's constitution, both of these agreements supersede domestic law.

Countries also implemented institutional changes that sought to assess pressures for protection with more neutral lenses than those used during the previous import substitution decades. In those decades, decisions were made through the interplay of interest group pressures and the arbitrary protectionist bureaucracy under an executive to whom Congress had delegated the administration of trade policies (Nogués and Baracat 2006). The direction of the institutional reform was toward objective, independent, and transparent procedures for assessing and implementing import policies.[18]

In the case of Argentina, the government introduced two important reforms. First, administration of the injury test, a key element in the new safeguards and antidumping legislation, was shifted away from the Ministry of Industry, where protectionist interests hold sway. The strategy that was adopted sought to replicate a salient characteristic of other countries' antidumping mechanisms: a separate track where the injury test would be assessed professionally and, as far as possible, isolated from political influences. Toward this objective, the National Commission on Foreign Trade (Comisión Nacional de Comercio Exterior, or CNCE) was created in 1994 under the Ministry of Economy.[19]

Second, the new rules and administrative regulations showed a clear bent toward an open economy, and in this regard, two reforms are worth mentioning. First, whether an injury had occurred would be decided by a vote of five CNCE commissioners on the basis of analytical and quantitative evidence. The CNCE implementing legislation (Decree 2121/94) also included clear wording in favor of such characteristics as lesser duty and a preference for short duration of antidumping measures. Furthermore, the CNCE began a tradition of calling public hearings that would provide a voice to third parties. The legislation also included a national interest clause that allowed the president or minister of economy to decide that no measures would be taken despite affirmative dumping and injury findings.

Nogués and Baracat (2006) argue that these reforms worked well in the sense of offering a relatively smooth and sensible operation of the political economy of trade liberalization in a country that had previously followed import substitution policies for decades. Until 2001–02, Argentina was certainly not among the Latin American countries that could be characterized as implementing few antidumping measures (Finger and Nogués 2006). Nevertheless, during the 1999–2002 recession, the new ways of administering barriers showed that with an increasingly overvalued currency and a convertibility strategy that had already lived its days, import policies could remain on track without derailing and returning to the traditional ways that had characterized the administration of import substitution policies in the past. At that point, things began to change.

Administrative Outcomes of the Antidumping Mechanism

During the late 1990s and up to early 2000s, the role of the CNCE was central in deciding which petitions deserved antidumping or safeguard protection. In contrast, given the strong preferences for import substitution, since the early 2000s, governments in Argentina have relaxed somewhat the criteria initially established by the CNCE.

Keeping this in mind and focusing exclusively on the average number of annual antidumping initiations presented in figure 3.3, we find, quite surprisingly, that fewer antidumping actions have taken place since the early 2000s than during the 1990s. Because of the impact of the international economic crisis, the average number of initiations increased during 2008 and 2009, but they were still well below the numbers recorded during the late 1990s. Between 1995 and 2001, initiations averaged 23.6 per year, whereas they fell to 14.9 per year between 2002 and 2010, although during 2011 they increased to 27.0.

The underlying significance of the numbers in figure 3.3 is very different for measures implemented until about 2001–02, and those since then. The more recent numbers should be assessed against three conditions. First, although WTO members have registered many complaints about Argentina's import licensing regime and other informal methods of import control, since 2001 only one instance of Argentina's application of antidumping measures was raised in the WTO dispute settlement process. Given the multiplicity of informal instruments

Figure 3.3 Antidumping Initiations per Year, 1995–2011

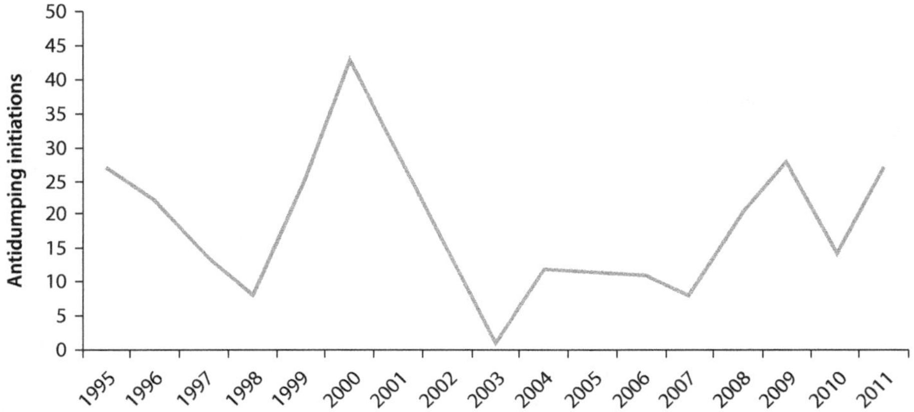

Sources: Data from WTO website on antidumping (http://www.wto.org/english/tratop_e/adp_e/adp_e.htm) and National Commission on Foreign Trade website (http://www.cnce.org).

Argentina has introduced, this single case suggests that antidumping application has been limited to instances where there was a clear legal basis under WTO rules. When the WTO legal basis for an antidumping restriction was questionable, other methods were applied. Second, as mentioned, the relatively lower average number of initiations should also be assessed against the high and sustained growth rates recorded by the economy in recent years in contrast to the recession years from 1999 to 2002. Third, administrative procedures and outcomes show other less visible but important differences between the functioning of the antidumping mechanism during the 1990s and the 2000s, including the following:

- *Public hearings.* During the 1990s, hearings were often held—not as an obligation but as a matter of administrative transparency—at the CNCE and were considered by the commissioners in the voting, but in recent years those hearings have been discontinued. The hearings, which were not required by the WTO agreement, represented a stage in the administrative process that was included in the regulations to give voice to potentially affected parties, including input users and consumers of final products. When a more protectionist version of the WTO agreements was adopted, potentially affected parties of contingent protection measures no longer had a voice in the decision-making process.

- *Lesser duty.* Lesser duty continues to be used intensively. But unlike during the 1990s, the reason now for this practice is to administer measures against China with greater care. China is not yet recognized as a market economy, and dumping margins on imports from China are usually found to be extremely high, but China's trade politics, including its subtle but firm retaliation responses, require focused prudence.

- *Duration.* Recent years have witnessed an increasing share of measures implemented for the maximum of five years allowed by the WTO rules. In contrast, during the 1990s, most measures were for two or three years, although the duration began increasing as the crisis deepened (Nogués and Baracat 2006).

- *National interest clause.* In a few instances, the national interest clause has been used to deal with possible retaliation from exporting countries (for example, the glyphosate imports from China in 2004 and of imports of Tramontina knives from Brazil in 2009). The original intention of the national interest clause was to give the government a degree of freedom to say no to the imposition of antidumping measures when it concluded that they would hurt downstream producers and consumers to a level considered unreasonable or that they were politically dangerous to the country's trade interests. The clause has now been used as a domestic political and legal cover for giving in to retaliation by trading partners. This use is another indicator that both Argentina and the exporter governments are resorting to the only instrument that was available before the rules-based GATT/WTO system was created: retaliation with trade restrictions against another country's trade restrictions. The original intent of the national interest clause was to allow an assessment of the impact on Argentine interests that would be harmed by the import restrictions. Peru, for example, in reforming its trade remedies, included an assessment of the impact on domestic users in parallel with the investigation of injury to domestic producers of competing products (Webb, Camminati, and Thorne 2006).

Target Countries

Imports from Brazil and China have been the main target of Argentina's antidumping measures and both countries have often requested and held conversations with the Argentine government about the application of such measures.[20] As will be discussed later, both countries have recently forcefully and quite successfully persuaded Argentina to reduce its import barriers on their exports. In 2004, Argentina and China arrived at an agreement in principle by which the country would be considered a "market economy" in antidumping investigations. Argentina, nevertheless, never implemented this agreement and, as discussed later, this failure to implement appears to be another important reason for China's retaliation.[21]

Import Coverage of Antidumping Measures

Argentina's import coverage of antidumping measures has declined quite significantly, from 1.9 percent in 2000 to 0.5 percent in 2010.[22] Estimates reported by Bown (2011) and Moore (2011) are similar to ours.

It is important to recall that imports of many products with antidumping measures have also been affected by other barriers, including NALs and, more recently, tight exchange controls.

As to the overall pattern of restrictions, during recent years, antidumping has been one of several instruments that Argentina has used to restrict imports. In contrast, during the liberalization years, the import control instrument was used to manage protectionist pressures in a manner consistent with the general thrust of trade policy—to integrate Argentina into the international economy. As currently used, trade remedies are instruments of a different economic philosophy that tends more to accommodate protectionist pressures than to manage them within a framework of integration into the international economy. Administrative decisions have moved closer to the protectionist side of the WTO antidumping agreement. Such dimensions as the elimination of public hearings, the longer duration of antidumping measures,[23] and a departure from regulatory preferences for lesser duties has had protectionist effects in relation to the 1990s. Finally, the CNCE is working within the politics of an import substitution government, and the antidumping mechanism is applied by commissioners who share this philosophy. As we demonstrated in *Fighting Fire with Fire* (Finger and Nogués 2006), there is considerable discretion within the rules-based GATT/WTO system. During the 1990s' liberalizations, this discretion was exploited in Argentina and in other countries toward the integration of these economies into the global economy—often applied to allow policy managers to choose *not* to apply restrictions even though the GATT/WTO criteria were met. Argentina is now in a decade in which this discretion is exploited in the service of a different economic philosophy. This change reflects one of the principal lessons of that study: the GATT/WTO system is a useful instrument for policy managers who want to liberalize, but it is not a rigid rule that requires such.

Industrial Promotion plus Import Protection for Tierra del Fuego

In addition to import protection, inefficient industries have been favored by other policies, such as preferential banking loans and fiscal incentives. A salient example is the incentives given to industrial production in Tierra del Fuego.

Since the military government initiated fiscal incentives for industrial promotion in 1972, the southernmost province of Argentina, the island of Tierra del Fuego, has benefited from those incentives. The incentives are principally for the assembly of parts brought in from outside. Law 19,640 exempts selected goods produced on the island from payment of all taxes. In November 2009, Congress passed Law 26,539, which increased the scope of the incentives by adding electronic products whose assembly would enjoy the exemptions. The law did this by raising tariffs and taxes for production in South America while exempting those from Tierra del Fuego—for example, for most electronic products the value added tax was raised from 10.5 percent to 21 percent (see article 3 of the law). Observers inform us that relative incentives created by Law 26,539 make production on the continent noncompetitive.

The response to these incentives on Tierra del Fuego has been quite impressive. For example, during 2009, 400,000 cellular phones were assembled on the island, but in 2010, the year following passage of the law, 4.9 million cellular phones were assembled. Meanwhile, imports of assembled electronic products were banned by NALs. For example, during 2008, imports of assembled units accounted for 98 percent of domestic sales of cellular phones, but more recently this share declined to about 20 percent (*Patagonia en Baires* 2011).

How important are the forgone taxes to the national and provincial treasuries? What are the costs to consumers? What has the impact been on employment creation and on the fiscal cost per job created?

Fiscal Subsidies to Tierra del Fuego

To offer an estimate of the fiscal costs, we need to know the number of finished products that would have been produced and imported in the absence of fiscal incentives and banned imports. To get that number, we assume that Argentina would have imported finished electronic products in an amount equal to the net increase of Tierra del Fuego's aggregate imports, because most of them correspond to electronic parts and components of electronic products. During 2009, imports into Tierra del Fuego amounted to US$802 million, whereas in 2010, the year following implementation of Law 26,539, the figure jumped to US$2.4 billion for a net increase of US$1.6 billion (Directorate General of Statistics and Censuses 2011, 35).

Assuming that the average tariff rate on these imports is 15 percent, forgone revenues of the national treasury would have amounted to US$240 million. A value added tax of 21 percent would have also been paid, generating an additional US$386 million. Under these assumptions, during 2010, the fiscal subsidies for assembling selected electronics on Tierra del Fuego would have amounted to a minimum of US$626 million. We say "at a minimum" because assembly facilities on Tierra del Fuego are also exempt from most other taxes (Law 19640), such as corporate income tax (at 35 percent) and internal taxes (a 17 percent rate on ex-factory prices), but these taxes are not included in our estimate of forgone revenues.

Consumer Cost

Assuming that imports of finished products are similar in quality to those assembled on the island—a big assumption—the consumer costs to Argentines can be estimated as the overprice they must pay for products whose imports are banned by licenses. In an attempt to offer an idea of how important these costs can turn out to be, we found a Blackberry model that is still sold in the United States and also assembled on Tierra del Fuego: Blackberry Curve 9300. Although this model sells for US$129.99 in the United States, it sells for Arg$1,999.00 or about US$411.00 (at the official exchange rate) in Argentina.[24] Another example is the iPad 2 (the 64-gigabyte model is not assembled on the island). In other countries, this item sells for US$575, whereas in Argentina it sells for about Arg$5,899, or US$1,215.[25]

Price differences of products have fluctuated quite significantly for many years. Today, control over imports of electronic products is more closely policed by the customs authorities than by other authorities. As a result, prices of electronics in Argentina are well above world prices, and recent legislation that favors Tierra del Fuego has much to do with those differences.

Fiscal Cost per Job Created

During 2010, manufacturing employment grew by approximately 2,800 jobs, or about 5 percent of the total employment on Tierra del Fuego (Directorate General of Statistics and Censuses 2011, 35; Ministry of Industry 2011d). Given the lower-bound estimate of the fiscal cost that we have documented, the fiscal subsidy per job created is, at a minimum, on the order of US$230,000 per year, or about Arg$1 million per year. This estimate compares with an average yearly labor cost on the island of approximately Arg$100,000–150,000 in 2011. Additional subsidies from internal and corporate income tax exemptions probably increase the fiscal subsidy per job quite significantly.

Therefore, nonlabor costs, including production inefficiencies, transport costs,[26] and extraordinary rents created by the Tierra del Fuego regime reveal a scheme that is draining the pockets of consumers and the coffers of the national and provincial governments.

Congressional Vote

Law 26,539 (the law that increased tax exemptions for Tierra del Fuego) was passed in the Congress's lower chamber (Cámara de Diputados) by 126 votes in favor, 7 votes against, and 54 abstentions. Given that under Argentina law about 50 percent of treasury revenues from the value added tax and the income taxes are shared with the provinces, their acceptance of a program in favor of Tierra del Fuego shows a high level of political support for industrial promotion.

Conclusion

No evident externality justifies this number of subsidies and protection to the electronic industry on Tierra del Fuego. The exemptions are not conditioned on the introduction of new processes or on research and development activities on Tierra del Fuego. The national components required by legislation to classify a Blackberry or other cellular brands as "made in Argentina" include a user's guide or manual, a product brochure, a warranty card, plastic bags, a case, packaging materials, and labeling.[27] The research and development in Blackberry cellular phones takes place in Canada, where the product was developed, and most manufacturing is outsourced to Asia. The incentives and the high cost of providing jobs through the incentive legislation have brought neither new technology nor other elements of the modern economy to Argentina.

Other Import Substitution Policies

Other policies are being implemented to reduce imports. For example, MERCOSUR countries have agreed to raise tariff rates of 100 eight-digit tariff lines of the MERCOSUR harmonized system. Furthermore, as the peso continues to appreciate, the government has decided to restrict the foreign exchange market by instituting severe controls. The discussion that follows offers a brief overview of these topics.

Exceptions to the MERCOSUR Common External Tariff

Under MERCOSUR, each member country is allowed to exclude 100 tariff lines from the common external tariff. In addition, in the most recent meeting of MERCOSUR presidents, which was held in December 2011, members agreed that on a temporary basis each country could increase tariff rates up to 35 percent in 100 additional lines beyond the existing common external tariff levels. As of mid-2012, each country was preparing its own list of candidate products, which would eventually require approval by the other members.[28]

The main justification that members of MERCOSUR offered for these adjustments was the injury threats associated with increases in international supplies triggered by the ongoing recessionary trends in the world economy. However, there is no requirement that these increases be preceded by an injury investigation, as prescribed by the WTO trade remedies agreements.

Intra-MERCOSUR trade, particularly between Argentina and Brazil, has also often been affected by sanitary and phytosanitary measures. Apparently, the governments have also placed informal pressures on major retail chain stores to source from domestic rather than foreign suppliers—another ad hoc instrument.

Foreign Exchange Controls

In early 2012, as a consequence of the increasing pressures associated with an overvalued currency, the government decided to tighten foreign exchange controls well beyond the levels that had been implemented until then. The control regime implemented by General Resolution 3252/2012 of the Federal Public Revenue Administration (Administración Federal de Ingresos Públicos, or AFIP). Titled "Anticipated Imports Sworn Statement," the resolution mandates that the foreign exchange needed to pay for each import be approved by specific government offices. As mentioned earlier, exchange controls cover all imports. They thus render superfluous the system of import licenses that has recently been dismantled.

Although approval is supposed be automatic according to this resolution, in practice such approval has not been the case, and newspaper articles are reporting that an increasing number of items cannot be found in the market. Profit remittances abroad are also being stopped, and the government is even requesting that profit funds already sent by companies in industries, such as insurance and mining, be repatriated.

Tight controls have also being extended to individuals and approval for purchasing foreign exchange is determined by the income flows declared to AFIP. Because 35 percent of the workforce is employed in informal jobs, these workers are automatically ineligible. Passengers traveling abroad must also request government clearance to buy foreign exchange at the official exchange rate. AFIP decides these requests on a case-by-case basis and in discretionary ways. For small purchasers, it makes no sense to appeal a negative decision by AFIP, because the burden of effort and the time spent are unreasonably high.

Regardless, there is evidence that legal complaints in the form of *recurso de amparo* are being filed. (*Recurso de amparo* is a relatively inexpensive legal form that can be used by citizens who feel that their constitutional rights have been violated.) And although the Supreme Court has not yet come to a decision, its president has declared that it will eventually do so (see, for example, *El Cronista* 2012).

Although it is too early to assess the extent to which these controls will affect import flows, the potential damage to trade is severe. Preliminary evidence shows that import growth is already decelerating, and strong complaints about Argentina's new controls from trading partners that signed the WTO statement (annex 3C) are being reported in newspapers. Consequently, domestic production is being disrupted, and imported consumer goods are disappearing from retail stores. These foreign exchange controls hold the potential of being more damaging to the economy than the NALs.

Newspaper Accounts of Domestic Impacts

Newspaper articles and other sources of independent news have reported some of the domestic impacts of the import substitution policies. For example, according to some reports, restaurants have voiced public complaints about the unavailability of Italian pasta and Chilean pink salmon (*Buenos Aires Delivery* 2012). A couple of news items illustrate the costly policy contradictions that evolve quite naturally in a disorganized import substitution policy such as Argentina's. A pro-government information source stated[29]:

> The interest of firms in producing on Tierra del Fuego is a clear indication that we are on the road toward establishing a national electronic industry. (Argentina .ar 2012)

More recently, and as a consequence of foreign exchange controls that have severely limited imports, including knock-down kit parts, the minister of industry and innovation of Tierra del Fuego stated that import controls are to blame for the loss of 4,000 jobs on the island (*La Mañana de Neuquén* 2012).

In May 2010, the following news was reported in Chile:

> The [Argentine] secretary of commerce has imparted *verbal* instructions to major retail stores, supermarkets, and minimarkets that they should refrain from importing among others the following products: canned corn .... Relatively import-intensive major retail stores, such as Jumbo, Carrefour, and Wal-Mart, are among the most affected. (*ProChile* 2010, emphasis added)

Newspapers have mentioned delays in landing imports:

> A World Bank report indicates that on average a firm invests 77 days in landing an import, a number that is higher than the 69 days invested by firms in Venezuela ... whereas in Brazil, Chile, and Mexico it takes 43, 23, and 16 days, respectively. (*Infobae* 2011)

In September 2011, several Argentine publishers were unable to obtain customs' release of almost 2 million books, many of which had been written and edited in Argentina but were shipped outside the country for printing. In separate meetings with government officials, each publishing company was told to provide a plan describing how it would have its printing done in Argentina in the future. The book scandal reached its climax in March 2012, when the government issued Resolution 453/10, which established additional technical regulations to minimize health risks associated with lead-based inks. The following is an excerpt from an interview with the president of Argentina's graphic industry (*La Nación* 2012a):

> **Question:** Do I run a risk in reading an imported book that was given to me as a gift?
> **Answer:** Assuming that the ink has no excessive lead, the answer is no.
> **Question:** But I don't eat the book, I just read it.
> **Answer:** Well, you also handle it and probably lick your finger over the ink in order to jump pages. This is a serious measure.

In another article on the same subject, *La Nación* (2012b) stated, "Now the import of books is forbidden."

On December 18, 2012, *Diario Perfil* reported that AFIP had trained dogs to smell and advise detect the existence of U.S. currency in suitcases: "The new elite 300 dogs have been trained to reduce the amount of dollar deposits that leave the country by US$30,000 million."

An editorial in a newspaper holding relatively liberal views stated that increasingly "industries are facing difficulties in finding inputs, consumers face a lack of several goods, doctors and hospitals are beginning work with inadequate instruments" (Jacquelin 2012).

Summing Up

President Kirchner and several of her ministers have left no doubt that their trade policy goal is import substitution. The antidumping mechanism introduced in the 1990s as part the integration of Argentine policy management into the GATT/WTO system has been redirected toward this objective. In addition, policy makers have expanded the menu of protectionist instruments to include less transparent policies, such as import licenses, countertrade arrangements, informal barriers (including telephone calls from government to business that leave no paper trail), and exchange controls have been used to reduce or stop imports.[30]

Table 3.3, at the beginning of this section, shows that Argentina has introduced more import restrictions than have most other countries and that the share of discretionary measures is high. Those measures have been complemented by industrial promotion incentives and other policies. We have presented Tierra del Fuego as an example. There are other measures that we have not discussed. Among them are special regimes for the shipbuilding industry, for imports of newsprint, for the editorial industry, for capital goods, and for several used products.

As has happened several times in the past, the exchange rate is being used as an anti-inflation anchor, and as the current account shrinks, severe foreign exchange controls have been instituted. A black market for foreign exchange has reappeared, and as this book goes to press, the gap with the official rate is growing rapidly and has already reached more than a 70 percent difference. Once again, Argentine economic governance has chosen short-term relief at the risk of serious negative long-term domestic and international impacts.

We have not looked into whether Argentine enterprises could seek redress under Argentine law when their businesses are harmed by the government's ad hoc measures and restrictions. We have found, however, no information in newspapers or other media of cases in which businesses have sought legal means to reverse possible administrative abuses. The lack of cases could be related to legal costs and time delays, as well as to fears of government retaliation. In contrast, in the case of the more recent controls on the allocation of foreign exchange, a number of legal appeals (*recursos de amparo*) regarding their constitutional basis have already been filed, but as yet there are no clear signals that the courts will limit this use of governmental discretion.

Agricultural Trade and Food Subsidy Policies

During the past decade, Argentina implemented particularly high export taxes on important cereal products. Tax rates reached a peak in mid-2008. Although they have declined since then for some products, they still stand at 23 percent for wheat, 20 percent for corn, and 35 percent for soybeans. Moreover, starting in early 2006, these barriers were reinforced with export bans on some products and export license requirements for bovine meats.[31] Finally, important fiscal subsidies have been provided to a group of food-processing firms.

This section reviews recent trends in export barriers, including taxes and QRs. Then, we summarize information on the magnitude of export taxation and food subsidies along with estimates of their impacts on domestic prices. The section concludes with comments on the political economy of export restrictions that help explain why, except during the 1990s, Argentina has heavily taxed agriculture since the 1940s.

Recent Policy Trends

Export Taxes

Shortly after the "big devaluation" that occurred in 2002, Resolution 11/2002 implemented export taxes on all products, although not at a uniform rate. Thereafter, successive announcements modified the original rates upward. Table 3.8 shows rapidly rising rates up to 2008 and a downward adjustment since then. The peaks are associated with the introduction of variable tax rates implemented by Resolution 125 of the Ministry of Economy in March 12, 2008, and

Table 3.8 Export Tax Rates, 2002–12
Percent

Resolution	*Issue date*	*Sunflower seeds*	*Soybeans*	*Wheat*	*Corn*	*Bovine meat*
Ministry of Economy 11	March 3, 2002	13.5	13.5	10.0	10.0	15.0
Ministry of Economy 35	April 8, 2002	23.5	23.5	20.0	20.0	15.0
Ministry of Economy 10	January 1, 2007	23.5	27.5	20.0	20.0	15.0
Ministry of Economy 368	November 9, 2007	32.0	35.0	28.0	25.0	15.0
Ministry of Economy 125 (introduced variable rates plan)[a]	March 12, 2008	41.0	41.0	33.0	24.0	15.0
Ministry of Economy 64	June 2, 2008	41.0	46.0	33.0	31.4	15.0
Ministry of Economy 80, 81, and 82	July 21, 2008	32.0	35.0	28.0	25.0	15.0
Ministry of Economy 26, 2008	December 23, 2008	32.0	35.0	23.0	20.0	15.0

Source: Data from Bolsa de Cereales (http://www.bolcereales.com.ar/).
a. These numbers are averages of the rates in place while Resolution 125/2008 was in effect.

eliminated shortly after in July of that same year. According to this scheme, which was applied to cereal exports, the rates varied positively with the level of international prices, which at the time were reaching peak values.[32]

During 2008, following the sudden increase in tax rates implemented by Resolution 125, residents across the countryside initiated a series of protests, and several national highways were blocked by trucks and agricultural machinery. The demonstrations succeeded, and in a historical outcome, Congress voted to dismantle variable taxation.

Despite its authority to fix commercial policies, faced with growing and dangerous social discontent, the government concluded that variable rates required by Resolution 125 needed stronger political support and submitted the resolution for congressional approval. Given that the voting on the floor was to a tie, the decisive vote had to be made by the president of the Senate, who was also the vice president of the country. The vice president voted against the resolution, and variable export taxes were eliminated shortly thereafter. The previous fixed rates once again went into effect. However, the vice president did not regain his previous influence, and in the 2011 presidential election, he was not chosen as the running mate.[33]

Although the tariff equivalent on several imported goods has been above the levels for export taxes reached under Resolution 125, no popular demonstration against these barriers has occurred. Likewise, there has been little social opposition to the quantitative export controls implemented since 2006. These barriers, as we examine later, imply ad valorem equivalent rates that at some points have been higher than those resulting from Resolution 125.

In midterm elections held in mid-2009, the government lost its majority in the lower chamber. Nevertheless, because of the governing party's continued majority in the Senate, the opposition could not advance its own agenda. Finally, in presidential elections held in October 2011, after the economy had recouped from the 2009 recession, the government won with 54 percent of the popular vote and regained control of both houses of Congress.

Quantitative Export Restrictions

As international food price increases accelerated from 2006 to 2008, QRs on exports began to be implemented, initially for bovine meat and wheat and more recently for corn. These products make up a significant part of the basic food basket and cost of living in Argentina.

As is the case with NALs, the levels of export quotas have been decided on an ad hoc basis. Argentina has no formalized procedures to govern either the determination of aggregate quota levels or their distribution among different Argentine exporters.

The absence of domestic law governing the application of export restrictions eliminates transparency and predictability in their application. Consequently, as addressed in chapter 5, accountability for trade policy decisions is a part of general political accountability rather than the regulatory accountability that increasingly characterizes trade policy governance in countries more integrated into the GATT/WTO legal system.[34] This situation adds to the uncertainties faced by agricultural producers. Both the price effects of controls and the uncertainty effects of when and by how much exports are restricted or taxed imply that the QR regime as applied in Argentina has been costly for many small and medium-size farms. For example, in comparison to the 2002 agricultural census, the census undertaken in 2009 shows a reduction of 57,000 farms, or 17 percent (*La Nación* 2009).

The export QRs are probably a factor explaining why the area planted in wheat has been declining. Of the total land planted in the three main cereals (wheat, corn, and soybeans) in 2006–07, when QRs against wheat exports began to be tightened, the shares of wheat and soybeans were 22 percent and 63 percent, respectively. For the 2009–10 planting season, these shares had changed to 13.7 percent and 71.8 percent, respectively. Soybean exports are free of export QRs, and therefore producer prices do not depend on arbitrary decisions.

The export restriction policies have generated significant quota rents or hidden export subsidies. For example, in the case of wheat, the average ad valorem equivalent of export QRs was around 17 percent.[35] Wheat mills are the other big beneficiaries of the implicit tax on primary producers, because the lower wheat price implies an input subsidy on the order of US$357 million. In short, the allocation of export quotas implies a major transfer of rents from farmers to exporters and wheat mills.

Food Subsidies

The National Office of Agricultural Trade Control (Oficina Nacional de Control Comercial Agropecuario, or ONCCA) is responsible for an extensive subsidy program for food processors. Table 3.9 provides a breakdown of how these subsidies were allocated among food-producing sectors. The numbers show that the largest amounts per approved subsidy have gone to dairy firms, chicken farms, and wheat mills in that order.

The sizes of the quota rents and food subsidies involved, along with the absence of clear and transparent rules for allocating export quotas and food

Table 3.9 Subsidy Authorizations, 2007–09

Product	*Number of authorizations*	*Value (US$)*	*Value per authorization (US$)*
Wheat flour	1,477	1,713,700,000	1,200,000
Corn flour	45	13,000,000	300,000
Dairy firms	181	615,900,000	3,400,000
Chicken farms	860	1,274,500,000	1,500,000
Milk producers	153,989	782,100,000	10,000
Wheat producers	25,613	338,600,000	10,000
Pigmeat producers	2048	89,400,000	40,000
Bovine feedlots	4,506	1,324,000,000	300,000
Other	778	11,800,000	20,000
Total	189,559	6,450,900,000	30,000

Source: Data from Bolsa de Cereales of Buenos Aires.

subsidies, have raised suspicions of fraud and corruption in the allocation of QRs and food subsidies. These suspicions prompted a proposal for congressional inquiry into the workings of the ONCCA, which was at that time responsible for administering the export quota and food subsidy programs. A document (Dictámen de la Cámara de Diputados 3797-D-10) was signed by congressional committees, including the Commission of Agriculture of the lower house of Congress. The title of the umbrella paragraph stating the objectives of the proposal to create an inquiry committee is as follows: "Knowledge and Investigation into Alleged Irregularities Surrounding the Functioning of the National Office of Agricultural Trade Control."

This investigation has resulted in no public report of findings. But on February 25, 2011, Decree 193/11 closed the ONCCA and replaced it with the Assessment and Coordination Unit of Subsidies for Domestic Consumption under the purview of the Ministry of Agriculture and the Ministry of Economy (*Conclave Político* 2011). The umbrella paragraph of Decree 193/11 states that it "is not appropriate for the functions of compensation, promotion, or development of (agricultural) activities through subsidies and refunds to be carried out by the same authority responsible for control of the same." However, this state of affairs had been going on for years.[36]

Export Barriers and Producer Prices

To what extent have export barriers distorted producer prices? To what extent have producer prices been reduced by QRs in relation to export taxes? The answers to these questions require an estimate of the ad valorem tax equivalent (AVE) of QRs. If we define the rate of total export taxation on product y as the sum of the legislated export tax rate (Et) plus the ad valorem equivalent rate of QRs (AVEy), then the fraction of the international free-on-board (FOB) price received by domestic producers (%FOBy) is given by

$$\%FOBy = 1 - Ety - AVEy = MPy/FOBy, \quad (3.1)$$

where MPy represents the market prices received by producers of y. Therefore,

$$AVEy = 1 - Ety - MPy/FOBy. \qquad (3.2)$$

Figure 3.4 shows monthly values of equation (3.1) from January 2004 to December 2010.[37] In addition to the very high levels of export taxation, the series shows the following characteristics: (a) a downward trend, meaning that as time has passed primary producers have received prices that are increasingly below international FOB prices; (b) the initial QR on wheat exports (a straightforward export ban) implemented in March 2006, which coincides with an increase in aggregate export taxation, only a fraction of which is accounted for by higher formal taxes; (c) increased producer price variability starting in early 2006; and (d) the negative impact on producer prices in the short time that Resolution 125 was in effect.

On average, to what extent have QRs reduced producer prices below the level determined by the formal export tax rates? Figure 3.5 shows monthly estimates of AVE, using equation (3.2), for the same three cereals. Clearly, since 2004, QRs have affected producer prices most significantly for wheat, although negative impacts on corn producers have been increasing. Soybean producers, by contrast, have been minimally affected by QRs; our

Figure 3.4 Ratio of Market Prices to Free-on-Board Prices for Wheat, Corn, and Soybeans, January 2004–December 2010

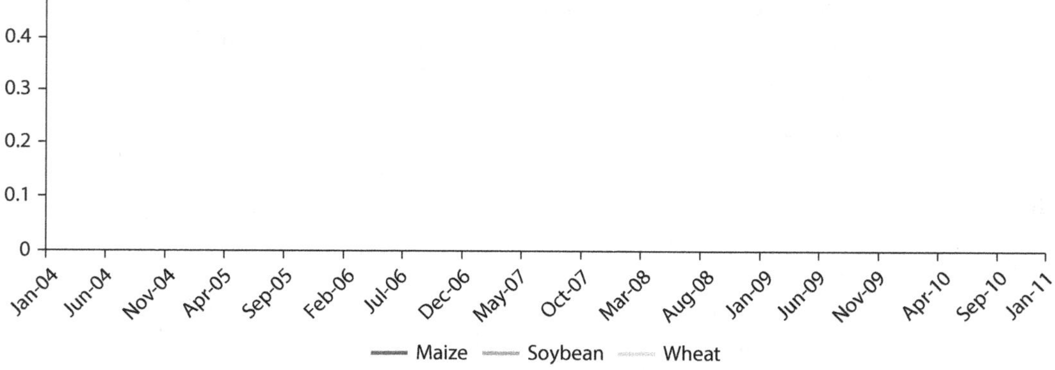

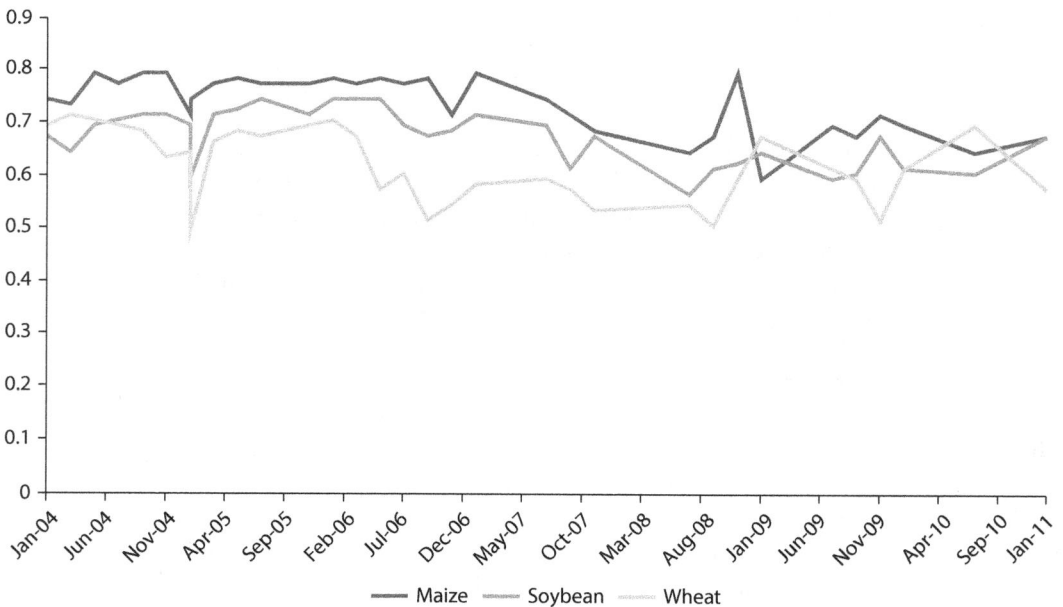

Source: Nogués 2011a.
Note: The initial ban on wheat exports was implemented in March 2006. Implementation of variable export taxes (through Resolution 125) took place on March 3, 2008. Variable export taxes were dismantled on July 18, 2008.

Figure 3.5 Ad valorem Equivalents of Quantitative Restrictions on Exports of Corn, Wheat, and Soybeans: Monthly Observations, 2004–10

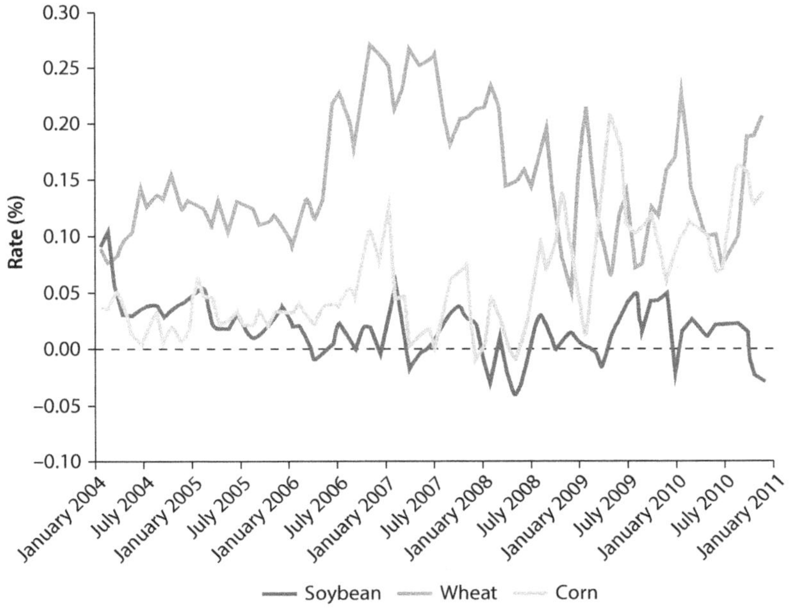

Source: Nogués 2011a.

interviews verify that, in fact, that soybean exports are practically free of these controls. Not surprisingly, as the area planted has been increasing, soybean exports have become the single most important tax-collecting product for the national treasury. Most of those taxes (70 percent), as we will discuss, do not fall within the general revenue-sharing formulas with the provinces.

Table 3.10 shows that between 2004–05 and 2006–10, the average rate of total export taxation increased quite significantly. Wheat increased from 29 percent to 40 percent, whereas corn increased from 24 percent to 29 percent. In contrast, for soybeans, the change in the average rate of total export taxation between both periods is relatively small. The last two columns show that for corn and wheat the proportional impact of export taxes in total taxation declined between both periods, meaning that the importance of export QRs in lowering producer prices increased.

Political Economy

Several political economic issues should be highlighted. First, there are four major umbrella organizations of primary agricultural producers: (a) Argentina Rural Society (characterized mainly by the relatively big landowners), (b) Argentine Agrarian Federation (representing small and medium-size

Table 3.10 Export Tax Rates and Aggregate Export Taxation for Wheat, Corn, and Soybeans: Averages of Monthly Observations, 2004–05 and 2006–10

	2004–05		*2006–10*		*Export tax rates as a percent of aggregate export taxation*	
Product	*Export taxes rate (%)*	*Aggregate export taxation[a] (%)*	*Export tax rate (%)*	*Aggregate export taxation[a] (%)*	*2004–05*	*2006–10*
Wheat	20.0	29.0	23.4	40.0	69.0	58.5
Corn	20.0	24.0	21.3	29.0	83.3	74.4
Soybeans	23.5	32.5	32.0	34.0	72.3	94.1

Source: Constructed from monthly data presented in Nogués 2011a.
Note: AVE = ad valorem tax equivalent.
a. Aggregate export taxation = Export tax + AVEs.

producers), (c) Argentine Rural Confederation, and (d) Coninagro (representing cooperative organizations). In a historical perspective, cohesive action by these organizations has been more the exception than the rule. But in mid-2008, guided by these organizations, the country united against Resolution 125 (Barsky and Dávila 2008). Since elimination of this resolution in July 2008, this unity has weakened significantly, although it could reappear if taxation against agriculture is further increased.

Second, export taxes have become the third most important source of treasury revenues after value added tax and income tax. For example, in 2008 export taxes falling on agricultural and agroindustrial exports represented 6.6 percent of treasury revenues and 1.7 percent of GDP (Nogués 2011a). On the political front, the importance of export taxes is heightened by the fact that, unlike the case with value added tax and income tax, distribution of proceeds is not regulated by automatic sharing rules. In contrast, most of these revenues are allocated at the president's discretion. This matter is of the greatest importance. Given the magnitude of the resources involved, this discretion has been a source of tensions between the central government and the provinces, particularly those that are major agricultural producers. The absence of binding sharing rules leads to discretion and political favoritism that, given the amount of taxes collected on primary exports, are probably standing at unprecedentedly high levels. This situation is another example of a significant departure from a rules-based government.

Third, export taxation has benefited processors, whose exports are taxed at much lower rates, to the detriment of primary producers. For example, the export tax rate on wheat is 23 percent, whereas it is 13 percent on wheat flour and 5 percent on wheat-based products such as pasta. Moreover, the export tax rate on corn is 20 percent, whereas on chicken exports, it is 5 percent. The export tax rate on soybeans is 35 percent, but a 32 percent rate applies to soybean oil and a 20 percent rate applies to biodiesel. Politically, this strong tax escalation can be traced to an unbalanced power structure. Thousands of dispersed primary producers with a weak ability to organize are poorly represented in contrast to a few concentrated processors and exporting firms that act cohesively. In any case, the evidence shows that taxation of agricultural exports has strengthened monopolistic and oligopolistic sectors.

Finally, it is interesting to note that WTO members have not found a way to successfully address opposition to agricultural export barriers. Several questions have been raised regarding Argentina's policies to no avail, and the country remains quite free from external pressures to reform: the country's trading partners can bark but not bite.

Some Conclusions

First, export duties and quotas have reduced the prices received by primary producers well below international prices. Second, primary producers are dispersed and are unable to organize to demand more equal treatment. Only in the extreme circumstance of the passage of Resolution 125 in early 2008 did they unite and speak out. Third, a 35 percent export tax on soybeans has apparently been assessed by primary producers as a safer planting bet than other crops that are affected by lower legislated rates but that are subject to arbitrary export QRs. As a result, the proportion of arable land allocated to soybeans has been increasing while that for wheat has been declining. And fourth, export quotas have skewed the distribution of risks against primary producers in favor of concentrated food processors and exporters that capture the bulk of QR rents.

Lessons from Multilateral and Bilateral Tensions

In this section, we first compare the policies and trade institutions that characterized the 1990s with those of the 2000s, paying attention to the role of the WTO and MERCOSUR regulations. We then offer brief comments on the apparent impact that bilateral threats have played in stimulating less protectionist enthusiasm. Two conclusions emerge. First, from the perspective of the domestic interests that bear the costs of these restrictions, the WTO and MERCOSUR institutions are wanting. Second, as a consequence, the threat of retaliation against the country has been an effective option for relatively big countries, but not for small ones such as Uruguay. Larger countries can press Argentina not to step beyond an understandable degree of protection.

WTO and Trade Policy Institutions

After five decades, the 1990s witnessed not only a return to more open trade policies but also, as mentioned earlier, the initial steps toward institutional reforms that sought to provide a higher degree of transparency to the implementation of trade policies.

Developments during 2002, however, were so extreme that the door opened for practically any socioeconomic experiment. The democratically elected president who had assumed office in late 1999 left power in December 2001 before ending his term, and in 2003, citizens elected a new president, Néstor Kirchner. He and his successor, Cristina Fernández de Kirchner, have reintroduced the import substitution strategy that characterized Argentine trade policy for several decades before the reforms of the 1990s.

In examining how Argentine trade policies have been addressed at the WTO, it is useful to differentiate between export barriers and import barriers.

Export Barriers

Argentina's experience is an important reminder of the very high costs associated with the failure of WTO negotiations to address agricultural export barriers. In effect, countries remain free to erect them as they see fit. Article XI of GATT 1994 bans quantitative export controls on agricultural products but allows temporary exceptions that seek to prevent critical food shortages. The WTO Agreement on Agriculture sought to limit this freedom but, from the experience of Argentina, without success. According to this agreement, countries imposing export barriers should give due consideration to the needs of importing countries. They should also give notice on the intention to introduce or raise these barriers. But during the 2007–08 peaks in world food prices when export bans proliferated, not one country provided notice (Hebebrand 2011). That circumstance is a significant example of WTO regulations that reflect good intentions but have no teeth.

The WTO agreements set no limits on the rate of export taxes. The existing constraint that the executive is now facing on this matter was achieved by the people and Congress, not by multilateral or regional obligations. As mentioned previously, such a limit was set during 2008 after the country was divided between those who were in favor and those who were against increasing agricultural taxation through variable export taxes. At the time, Congress voted against this policy, and the executive was forced to replace the variable mechanism with the previous fixed ad valorem rates. This social behavior represents the salient trade policy constraint on exports—and trade policy generally—that the executive has faced in recent years. It put the government on notice regarding excessive taxation on agriculture.

Regarding export QRs, possible corruption in their allocation by the ONCCA triggered domestic political action. The efficiency effects and overall cost to the Argentine economy have not been the basis for political concern. During 2010, some congressional committees initiated the first steps toward an inquiry that would have eventually led to a parliamentary debate on whether the administration of export QRs and food subsidies had been tainted by corruption. Perhaps in response, the government—as noted earlier—assigned responsibility for administering the export quota and food subsidy programs to a different agency. This incident is a reminder that well-intentioned but discriminatory and nontransparent administration of government controls creates an opportunity for corruption, can trigger suspicions of corruption regardless of whether it actually takes place, and can make the policing of corrupt practices difficult.[38]

Import Barriers

Also on the import side, the protectionist impetus of Argentina has for the time being remained free of effective international pressures for reform. It is important here to distinguish between NALs and contingent protection. Earlier, we presented a list of administrative changes that shifted antidumping measures toward increasing levels of protection although the average number of initiations has declined since the 1990s. In appearance at least, these measures were administered through the relatively transparent process that we summarized and that is described more precisely by Nogués and Baracat (2006).

Also, through an increasing number of tariff lines, imports are now being restricted through NALs, which have been administered in a way that adds to the restrictive effect of the measures. Likewise, the lack of the procedures' transparency makes opposition more difficult. It restores the bias toward concentrated producer interests versus diffused user interests—a bias that has historically produced excessive import restrictions and that the rules structure of the now abandoned procedures introduced in the 1990s had attempted to eliminate.

So far, no forceful multilateral or domestic action has occurred to correct the arbitrary and discretionary administration of this policy or the more recently established foreign exchange controls. Since 2004, at the WTO Committee on Import Licensing, members have been increasingly critical of NALs implemented by Argentina, but until the recent complaint under the WTO Dispute Settlement Understanding, these pressures have remained within the Council on Trade in Goods and the more technically oriented Committee on Import Licensing. The recent statement from the council (supported by many developing and developed members) and the Dispute Settlement Understanding complaint by the EU might signal that things are changing. However, there has already been a long lag between action by Argentina and the response of the WTO system.

Domestically, it is interesting to note that instead of demanding reform, enterprises (national and international alike) that have been pressed by the government for approval of NALs in exchange for achieving import substitution targets or compensating exports have agreed to do things in a new way (or revert to an old way) characterized by a command-and-control process instead of demanding greater transparency of government decisions.

In a nutshell, Argentina has taken significant steps toward reversing an important trade liberalization effort implemented during the 1990s. Statements by the president leave no room for doubts regarding the final objective: (a) "We have to deepen import substitution" (Losauro 2011); (b) "import substitution implies more jobs for Argentineans" (Informe Urbano 2010); and (c) if possible, domestic production has to substitute imports to an extent that not even construction nails will be imported ("Ni un clavo importado, si fuera posible") (Delletorre 2011).

Unlike the past, the government is now bound by international and regional obligations, including a multilateral commitment not to raise tariffs above

35 percent and a regional commitment to the common external tariff of MERCOSUR. One would have hoped that these and other WTO and regional obligations would have introduced more rationality into trade policies. Nevertheless, so far the government has found loopholes and has exploited the slowness or weakness of the disciplinary procedures of these agreements. Except for a few bilateral actions, which we will describe, the country has escaped major consequences.[39] One would have hoped that the multilateral obligations that were signed into domestic law would have put a limit on policies restricting imports, but they have not. Argentina is likely the country currently holding the trophy for demonstrating that when all is said and done, the only significant constraint on protectionism is domestic politics. On this subject, Finger (2012, 435) states, "The discipline in the system is less a matter of how the WTO regulates, more a matter of how the WTO has helped to shape the evolution of the domestic institutions that regulate."

Bilateral Tensions and Retaliation

The most forceful points of resistance to Argentina's ways of administering commercial policies have been Brazil and China, which have used methods that do not raise objections regarding how policies are made but only regarding the impact of measures. The following actions illustrate how, without making international noise, these two big countries have forced Argentina to lower its restrictions against their exports.

Brazil

On February 15, 2011, the Argentine government published Resolution 45, announcing that "given that there have been significant changes in automobile imports, foreign trade flows require an evaluation." Furthermore, the resolution stated that the government was moving toward requiring "the previous approval of nonautomatic import licenses." Most imported cars come from Brazil under a special MERCOSUR agreement. Such a unilateral action by Argentina triggered a series of responses from Brazil that ranged from complaints to retaliation through the implementation in early May 2011 of NALs for cars imported from Argentina—tit for tat.

Argentina and Brazil have had permanent trade tensions associated probably more with the wide fluctuation of their bilateral exchange rates than with trade policies. Argentina is an important and strategic trade partner of Brazil, and nothing suggests that this state of affairs will change any time soon. The MERCOSUR customs union notwithstanding, Argentina can stop goods at the border, not always with a reasonable justification under the MERCOSUR agreement, and Brazil can act likewise. Interviews suggest that tensions in the auto trade have not yet been normalized. And given the existing level of uncertainty in international trade flows, it is likely that normalization will take time. In the meantime, an important share of bilateral trade flows remains managed—a situation that represents still another example of moving away from a rules-based trade system.

China

Between April and October 2010, China banned soybean oil imports from Argentina, alleging the existence of chemical residues that exceeded agreed standards. Although this ban lasted, China redirected imports toward other sources, most notably Brazil and the United States. Argentina had to seek other export markets, such as India. By some estimates, during the ban, prices paid for Argentina's exports declined by US$50–70 per ton for an aggregate loss of about US$300 million (see, for example, Longoni 2010).

To our knowledge, there has never been a clear explanation of what precisely triggered the import ban by China. Most observers agree that if a problem really existed, Argentina had the resources and technological capability to implement the adjustments required by China in a short time.[40] Nevertheless, the ban lasted several months. When it was finally lifted, Argentina's Ministry of Agriculture announced that such a decision was made thanks to a presidential visit to China in July 2010.

The facts suggest that the sanitary ban was a subtle retaliation implemented after the failure of informal bilateral talks to convince Argentina to reduce its enthusiasm for erecting barriers against imports from China. During the past decade, China has been an increasing target of Argentina's antidumping measures, and on this count, the retaliation was successful: Argentina initiated 18 antidumping investigations against China during 2009, but only 3 in 2010 and 2 in the first half of 2011.

Concluding Remarks

On October 25, 2011, Cristina Fernández de Kirchner was reelected president with 54 percent of the popular vote; her party also regained majority in both houses of Congress. The extent to which the economy should be open or closed was not a theme during the presidential campaign. Import barriers and, more generally, the degree of openness of the economy were never issues of debate. The one candidate who spoke openly in favor of eliminating export barriers received less than 2 percent of the vote. As a consequence and by default, the election outcome endorsed both the new restrictions and the new forms through which they had been imposed during the past decade.

The new trade strategy runs through discretionally administered processes that have been centralized to a point where all imports now require government approval. This strategy has been going on for several years despite the country having signed the WTO agreements. The ineffectiveness of multilateral legal challenges against these policies suggests that the country's international legal obligations have not constrained its choice of trade policies. The more significant constraints have come more from bilateral retaliatory actions taken by large countries such as Brazil, China, and more recently the United States.

Internally, the experience with Resolution 125, which instituted variable export taxes, and the social discontent that the resolution triggered are an example of the domestic problems that the absence of a rules-based government can produce. A related lesson is that if arbitrary management of trade policy is the preferred government policy, then a rules-based international system is likewise compromised. International trade relations revert to the more primitive politics of (threats of) retaliation, as the examples of Brazil and China have shown.

In hindsight, the origins of Argentina's policy and institutional shift in the 1990s toward greater openness can best be explained by the declining returns of import substitution policies and the inefficiencies and inflation (at points hyperinflation) that have accompanied them. The retrogression was so painful, that for once in their lifetimes, people said "enough is enough" and voted for change in the 1990s. Nevertheless, the 2001–02 crisis and the subsequent return of good times associated with a significant improvement in the country's terms of trade made room for populist policies. People's preferences shifted once again toward their more traditional beliefs that governments, more than hard work, can improve their lives.

Argentina's experience during the past eight decades is not a path toward sustainable development but a sum of short-run experiences where political gains always predominate over a shift toward a rules-based system under the constitution. This experience suggests that shifting social preferences toward another opportunity for implementing an open economy and inclusive society will likely take quite some time and perhaps another crisis.

Annex 3A: Trade Flows by Origin or Destination and Type of Goods

Important shifts have taken place in the origin and destination of aggregate trade flows. Table 3A.1 shows that during the 1990s, unilateral trade liberalization policies in neighboring countries, plus the formation of MERCOSUR, greatly increased the importance of the MERCOSUR agreement in the trade flows of Argentina, whereas its trade shares with the member states of the North American Free Trade Agreement (NAFTA) and the EU declined. In contrast, during the 2000s, trade has increased most rapidly with China and with other countries, including the Andean countries, India, and Mexico.

In 2010, trade with these other countries explained the major part of Argentina's surplus and, together with trade with the EU, more than compensated the increasing deficits with China, MERCOSUR, and the NAFTA countries. Given the increasing value of Brazil's currency during most of those years and the significant real devaluation of the peso, the switch in the bilateral balance from a surplus in the 1990s to a deficit in the 2000s is quite telling of the relative strength of structural reforms in the two countries.

Tables 3A.2 and 3A.3 present exports and imports by broad product groups. We highlight a couple of issues. First and most important, the numbers in table 3A.2 indicate a significant decline in the share of fuels in total exports from 19 percent in 2000 to 10 percent in 2010. As a consequence of relatively stagnant exports in a context of rapid growth and increasing overvaluation, the fuel and energy trade balance went from a surplus of US$3.792 billion in 2000 to a deficit of US$2.931 billion in 2011. Declining growth rates of fuel exports are

Table 3A.1 Exports and Imports by Origin and Destination: 1990, 2000, and 2010

Exports and imports	*MERCOSUR*	*China*	*European Union*	*NAFTA members*	*Others*	*Total*
Exports						
1990 (US$ millions)	1,833	241	3,796	2,068	4,415	12,353
2000 (US$ millions)	8,394	879	4,598	3,739	8,641	26,341
2010 (US$ millions)	17,294	6,117	11,185	6,285	27,253	68,134
Change, 2000/1990 (%)	358	265	21	81	96	113
Change, 2010/2000 (%)	106	596	143	68	215	160
Imports						
1990 (US$ millions)	833	32	1,124	954	1,134	4,077
2000 (US$ millions)	7,197	1,219	5,758	5,630	5,344	25,148
2010 (US$ millions)	18,968	7,678	9,762	8,351	11,743	56,502
Change, 2000/1990 (%)	764	3709	412	490	371	517
Change, 2010/2000 (%)	164	530	70	48	120	125
Trade balance						
1990 (US$ millions)	1,000	209	2,672	1,114	3,281	8,276
2000 (US$ millions)	1,197	−340	−1,160	−1,891	3,297	1,103
2010 (US$ millions)	−1,674	−1,561	1,423	−2,066	15,510	11,632

Source: Data from National Institute of Statistics and Censuses and Foreign Affairs Ministry.
Note: Member countries are Canada, Mexico, and the United States. NAFTA = North American Free Trade Agreement.

Table 3A.2 Exports by Sector, 1990, 2000, and 2010

Exports	*Agricultural and minerals*	*Agricultural-based manufactures*	*Other manufactures*	*Fuels and energy*	*Total*
1990 (US$ millions)	3.175	4.828	3.364	985.000	12.353
2000 (US$ millions)	5.346	7.864	8.230	4.902	26.341
2010 (US$ millions)	15.142	22.661	23.816	6.515	68.134
Change, 2000/1990 (%)	68	63	145	398	68
Change, 2010/2000 (%)	183	188	189	33	183

Source: Data from National Institute of Statistics and Censuses and Foreign Affairs Ministry.

Table 3A.3 Imports by Type of Goods, 1990, 2000, and 2010

	US$ millions			*Change (%)*	
Import groups	*1990*	*2000*	*2010*	*2000/1990*	*2010/2000*
Capital goods	636	5,924	11,647	832	97
Intermediate goods	2,069	8,443	17,687	308	110
Fuels	322	1,035	4,474	221	332
Parts	691	4,449	11,459	544	158
Consumption goods	330	4,609	6,611	1,295	43
Autos	12	799	4,482	6,706	461
Other goods	17	23	142	33	525
Total	4,077	25,280	56,502	520	123

Source: Data from National Institute of Statistics and Censuses.

in sharp contrast with their rapid growth and increasing export share during the 1990s, when the sector was deregulated and privatized. This decreasing performance of the fuel and energy trade sector is also related to policies that have subsidized domestic consumption by taxing exports heavily. For example, exports of crude petroleum are taxed at a rate of 45 percent, and natural gas is taxed at an even higher rate.

These policies have implied lower rates of investment and exploration and declining reserves, which have put increasing pressure on the trade balance. Declining investment in exploration and declining rates of production growth have been used by the same government to justify expropriation of YPF (Yacimientos Petrolíferos Fiscales), the country's biggest oil company. Expropriation of YPF was approved by law. In the Senate, the bill passed with 63 votes for, 4 votes against, and 3 abstentions, whereas in the House it passed with 207 votes for and 36 against. The experience suggests that the future of fuel and energy output under government control does not look bright.

Additionally, the growth in exports of other manufactures, which generally include the most protected industries, is primarily explained by the trade in autos, which mainly takes place between Argentina and Brazil and is protected by special MERCOSUR rules (see, for example, WTO 2007). There is no clear indication that international competitiveness of these other manufactures has increased in recent years.

Finally, a brief summary of imports by broad type of goods is presented in table 3A.3. The table shows that the slowest increase during the past decade was in consumption and capital goods imports, whereas during the 1990s, those groups were dynamic. This situation reflects the lower rate of investment, particularly foreign direct investment, that has accompanied the increasingly inward-looking, centralized, and discretionary policies of recent years.

Annex 3B: Import Coverage of Nonautomatic Licenses

NALs against houseware imports were first issued in 2004 (Resolution 444) and included products such as heaters, water heaters, gas kitchen appliances, and freezers. More recently, since 2008, the list of housewares under NALs was extended to include washing machines, electric kitchen appliances, video monitors and projectors, air conditioners, radios, and televisions (table 3B.1).

As table 3B.1 indicates, the share of imports subject to NALs in total houseware imports decreased from 33.9 percent in 2007 to 27.3 percent in 2010. Imports of housewares subject to NALs declined by 33.0 percent, whereas imports of housewares that were not subject to NALs declined by only 7.0 percent during the 2007–10 period.

In relation to total imports, the share of houseware imports subject to NALs declined from 1.4 percent in 2007 to 0.8 percent in 2010. These figures can be viewed as a rough indication that NALs against houseware imports have resulted in what the government expected: a reduction of imports and increased protection to domestic production.

Table 3B.1 Share Indicators of Houseware Imports, 2007–10

Indicator	*2007*	*2008*	*2009*	*2010*
I. Imports of 4-digit lines that include housewares (US$ thousands) (II + III)	1,832,068	2,032,786	1,211,723	1,516,487
II. Imports of houseware products subject to nonautomatic licenses (US$ thousands)	621,019	696,535	348,024	414,242
III. Houseware imports of 4-digit lines not subject to NAL (US$ thousands)	1,211,049	1,336,251	863,699	1,102,245
IV. Total imports (US$ thousands)	44,441,163	57,151,309	38,493,104	50,756,470
II/I (%)	33.9	34.3	28.7	27.3
II/III (%)	51.3	52.1	40.3	37.6
II/IV (%)	1.4	1.2	0.9	0.8

Source: Data from official import statistics.

Annex 3C: Joint Statement of Several WTO Members on Argentina's Import Restricting Policies and Practices

The complete joint statement reads as follows:

> Argentina's Import Restricting Policies and Practices: Joint Statement by Australia, the European Union, Israel, Japan, Korea, Mexico, New Zealand, Norway, Panama, Switzerland, Chinese Taipei, Thailand, Turkey, and the United States
>
> Council for Trade in Goods
> March 30, 2012
>
> We would like to express jointly our continuing and deepening concerns regarding the nature and application of trade-restrictive measures taken by Argentina, which are adversely affecting imports into Argentina from a growing number of WTO Members.
>
> These measures include the overly broad use of non-automatic import licensing trade balancing requirements, and pre-registration and pre-approval of all imports into Argentina.
>
> Since 2008, Argentina has greatly expanded the list of products subject to non-automatic import licensing requirements. Currently, an import license is required for approximately six hundred 8-digit tariff lines in Argentina's non-agricultural goods schedule. The products affected include, but are not limited to, laptops, home appliances, air conditioners, tractors, machinery and tools, autos and auto parts, plastics, chemicals, tires, toys, footwear, textiles and apparel, luggage, bicycles, and paper products.
>
> A non-automatic licensing requirement is WTO incompatible unless it is necessary to implement measures which are imposed in conformity with the relevant WTO rules and does not have trade-restrictive or trade-distortive effects on imports beyond those caused by the underlying restriction. The non-automatic licensing requirement must comply with all relevant provisions of the Agreement on Import Licensing Procedures, including a maximum processing period of 60 days.

Companies from many of the Members that support this statement report that Argentina's non-automatic import licensing scheme has a trade-restrictive effect on imports and that there are long delays in the issuance of import licenses. Many companies have reported wait periods of up to six months and longer. In some instances, companies are denied import licenses altogether, without justification or explanation.

The lack of transparency in Argentina's implementation and administration of its import licensing regime creates profound uncertainty both for exporters and potential exporters to Argentina, as well as for investors in Argentina.

In January 2012, Argentina announced regulations that went into effect on February 1, requiring pre-registration, review, and approval of each and every import transaction. These regulations are creating long delays and resulting in huge costs for many of the exporters from Members supporting this statement.

It appears that this new system is operating as a *de facto* import restricting scheme, on all products.

Argentina has made clear through public government statements that it has also adopted an informal "trade balancing" policy, whereby companies seeking to import products must agree to export, dollar for dollar, goods of an equal or greater value or establish production facilities in Argentina.

Many companies have reported receiving telephone calls from Argentine government officials in which they are informed that they must agree to undertake such trade balancing commitments prior to receiving authorization to import goods.

The Ministry of Industry's website is replete with press releases announcing these trade balancing and domestic production arrangements. These arrangements include well-known automakers agreeing to export products such as wine, olive oil, and soy meal, and requiring companies across a number of sectors to undertake production in Argentina without reference to the economics of doing so.

Argentina may claim that companies enter into these arrangements voluntarily, but many of the Members supporting this statement share concerns that it may be operating otherwise.

We are not aware of any official directive or resolution setting out these trade balancing or investment requirements. However, high-level Argentine government officials have been quoted in the Argentine press as saying quite clearly that the purpose of these requirements is to improve its trade balance by restricting imports and promoting exports.

Many of the Members that support this joint statement today have previously raised concerns about Argentina's increasingly protectionist measures both bilaterally and multilaterally beginning in 2008 when Argentina began progressively expanding the number of products subject to its non-automatic import licensing requirements.

Concerns have been raised and questions have been directed to Argentina in the Committee on Import Licensing, the Committee on Agriculture, and in this Council. However, Argentina has failed to adequately address these concerns or respond to Members' questions.

Indeed, rather than eliminating these import-restrictive measures and practices, Argentina has introduced new measures, and the existing measures have become increasingly problematic for our exporters.

The import-restrictive measures and practices that Argentina has put in place are unbefitting any WTO Member, particularly a member of the G-20 who has committed to refrain from raising new barriers to trade and investment. In light of the shared goal of making every effort to sustain global economic growth, Argentina's measures, which clearly limit the growth-enhancing prospects for trade, are particularly troubling.

We Members who support this Joint Statement request that Argentina take immediate steps to address the concerns we have raised today, and that many Members have raised in the past, by removing or terminating these import-restrictive measures and practices.

If, on the other hand, despite the concerns described above, Argentina continues to maintain these import-restrictive measures and practices, Argentina should provide a detailed written explanation of why in its view these measures and practices are consistent with WTO rules. Members reserve their rights to pursue this matter further.

Notes

1. The government of President Arturo Frondizi (1958–62) and military regimes of 1966–69 and 1976–82 introduced minor relaxations of protectionist restrictions, the latter under a highly overvalued currency.
2. The policy program of that regime had built-in seeds for failure: a macroeconomic policy that led to a severe overvaluation of the peso and an extended and powerful monopolistic military industrial complex that was sheltered from the preannounced program of tariff reductions being applied to the rest of the economy.
3. These views have been elaborated by several prominent authors, such as Ferrer (1983), who was minister of economy.
4. Billmeier and Nannicini (2009) provide an overview of the relevant literature.
5. Recent contributions by Anderson, Lloyd, and MacLaren (2007) and Sturzenegger and Salzani (2007), using similar methodologies, offer comparative estimates of degrees of protection of these two countries.
6. The primary function of such institutions is to shift resources from one interest group to another rather than to provide an environment that stimulates the creation of new wealth.
7. In contrast, more recently foreign direct investment has remained low and capital flight high.
8. Estimates of capital flight diverge, but according to an article published in *Clarín* (2011), although capital flight reached US$11.41 billion during 2010, the accumulated figure was already standing at US$15.00 billion by August 2011.
9. Except for the years 2007–10 when the official price deflator had become unreliable, we use estimates of the real exchange rate published by the Central Bank of Argentina and constructed on the basis of a trade-weighted basket. See Central Bank of Argentina, May 2005, http://www.bcra.gov.ar/pdfs/indicadores/TCRMMetodologia.pdf.

10. According to some newspapers, the reasons for this change may not all be related to the goal of centralization. A recent accusation published in newspapers indicated that corruptive practices in the administration of import licenses might have taken place; therefore, the new administrative arrangements could be a way of minimizing these risks. See, for example, De Santis (2011). In April 2012, partly as a consequence of suspicion of corruptive practices in the administration of licenses, the secretary of industry resigned (Kanenguiser 2012).
11. The Uruguay Round agreements, including that for import licenses, were incorporated through Law 24,425 into national legislation.
12. The late 1990s also witnessed an increase in agricultural protection by some member countries of the Organisation for Economic Co-operation and Development with negative consequences on efficient exporters like Argentina.
13. Since this chapter was drafted, most NALs have been dismantled through Resolution 11/2013. This decision must be related to the WTO dispute against Argentina listed by the WTO as "Measures Affecting the Importation of Goods." The complaint was endorsed by several countries and was triggered by NALs and other import barriers. Despite the dismantling of NALs, the dispute against Argentina continues, based now on barriers administered through foreign exchange controls implemented earlier through Resolution 3252/2012. (These resolutions are discussed later in this chapter.) In light of these later controls, the dismantling of NALs is presumed to have minimal effects on imports. Given the lengthy duration of NALs without serious multilateral and regional challenges associated with the significant import substitution effects that they have had in Argentina, we have considered of interest to leave the analysis as initially drafted.
14. Nogués and Baracat (2006) show that during the few years that Argentina managed an open economy, some of these products received antidumping protection, safeguard protection, or both.
15. Of these lines, 374 are also covered by automatic licenses. This juxtaposition could be the consequence of administrative oversight, but it could also become a potential double lock on imports in the event that NALs have to be suspended or reformed along lines that resemble WTO obligations more closely.
16. Imports have also been stopped through government telephone calls to businesses.
17. It should also be noted that the latest trade policy review of Argentina (published in 2007) did not flag NALs as a delicate trade policy topic.
18. At the time, export barriers had practically been dismantled and remained that way during most of the 1990s. This significant unilateral measure has often gone unnoticed.
19. Toward its goal of sheltering the CNCE from interest group pressures, the executive informally tested the possibility of having Congress approve it as an independent office. Nevertheless, the executive considered the odds to be against independence, and the proposal was never formally submitted.
20. Moore (2011) presents a time series of measures and import coverage indicators of antidumping actions.
21. This issue has since been discussed in several newspaper articles (for example, *La Voz* 2010).
22. We are grateful to Francis Ng for these computations.
23. Moore (2011, 335, figure 9.3) shows a steady decline after 2001 in the share of antidumping orders removed before the five-year WTO limit was reached.

24. Price information came from the websites of N1 Wireless and Frávega. Information was accessed on December 7, 2012.
25. Price information came from the websites of Amazon and Frávega. Information was accessed on December 7, 2012.
26. Electronic knock-down kit parts enter through the port of Buenos Aires and then travel 3,000 kilometers to Tierra del Fuego. After assembly has been completed, they travel another 3,000 kilometers to arrive close to the major consumer markets in continental Argentina.
27. See Resolution 245/2009, which is available at http://www.infoleg.gov.ar/infolegInternet/anexos/155000-159999/156463/norma.htm.
28. Since this chapter was drafted, the MERCOSUR countries have implemented this agreement, in the case of Argentina through Decree 25/2013. The list of products covers several that in recent years have been highly protected through other policies, such as antidumping measures and NALs, including toys, clothing, footwear, housewares, and electronics.
29. The quotations in this section were translated by the authors from Spanish.
30. For example, an editorial published by *La Nación* on November 19, 2011, stated that the secretary of domestic trade communicated through phone calls to fertilizers and agrochemical companies that they should refrain from importing.
31. Analysis of the impact of quantitative restrictions on bovine meat exports is presented in Nogués and Porto (2007).
32. Export taxes had previously been increased in early November 2007 (*La Opinión* 2007). In both instances, the measures were supported by political statements in favor of reducing the impact on consumer costs that growing international prices were having. At the time the variable export levies were implemented, the following increases in international prices had taken place during the previous six months: (a) soybean, 66 percent; (b) sunflower seeds, 91 percent; (c) maize, 39 percent; and (d) wheat, 38 percent.
33. The vice president's brief words can be seen on YouTube (http://www.youtube.com/watch?v=i7fZ0pm29lM).
34. The application of export taxes has never come under GATT/WTO discipline. Although the system prohibits QRs on exports as well as on imports, it allows export taxes and imposes no procedural requirements. Likewise, export taxes have never been a part of the GATT negotiating process. Hence, the GATT/WTO system has never applied the disciplines of reciprocity and bindings to their application.
35. This calculation is shown later in table 3.10. It is the difference between the rate of aggregate export taxation (40.0 percent) and the formal export tax rate (23.4 percent).
36. The most serious published inquiry into the behavior of the ONCCA is Longoni (2011).
37. Our estimates are based on international prices and export tax rates from the website of the Ministry of Agriculture (http://www.minagri.gob.ar/), whereas MPy represents auction prices published by the Buenos Aires Futures and Options Exchange (http://www.matba.com.ar/). Auctions are for deliveries at different dates in the future. We use deliveries for the same week or month, which are believed to better correspond with the spot FOB prices published daily by the Ministry of Agriculture.
38. Although the government has shifted the administration of export quotas and food subsidies, it has done so without issuing a formal report on the findings

of the inquiry commission appointed to review the matter. The absence of a report, in itself, is a step backward from the procedural reforms of the 1990s and could raise concern about the transparency of the process of evaluating the organizations in question and the accountability to which administrators have been held.

39. Argentina has been taken to the WTO dispute settlement body on 17 occasions, but only twice for measures implemented after 2001: one for a presumed violation of the antidumping agreement and the other for a countervailing measure against olive oil imports from the EU.
40. Argentina is known for having one of the most modern vegetable oil–producing technologies in the world.

References

Acemoglu, Daron, and James Robinson. 2012. *Why Nations Fail: The Origins of Power, Prosperity, and Poverty*. New York: Crown.

Anderson, Kym, Peter Lloyd, and Donald MacLaren 2007. "Distortions to Agricultural Incentives in Australia Since World War II." *Economic Record* 83 (263): 461–82.

Argentina.ar. 2012. "Computadoras tablets en Tierra del Fuego." January 22.

Barsky, Osvaldo, and Mabel Dávila. 2008. *La rebelión del campo: Historia del conflicto agrario argentino*. Buenos Aires: Editorial Sudamericana.

Bertello, Fernando. 2011. "John Deere instalará una planta de tractores y cosechadoras en el país". *La Nación*, September 26.

Billmeier, Andreas, and Tommaso Nannicini. 2009. "Trade Openness and Growth: Pursuing Empirical Glasnost." *IMF Staff Papers* 56 (3): 447–75.

Bolsa de Comercio de Córdoba. 2010. *El Balance 2010 de la Economía Argentina*. Córdoba, Argentina: Bolsa de Comercio de Córdoba. http://www.bolsacba.com.ar/investigaciones/balance-de-la-economia.

Bown, Chad P., ed. 2011. *The Great Recession and Import Protection: The Role of Temporary Trade Barriers*. Washington, DC: World Bank. http://www.cepr.org/pubs/books/CEPR/great_recession_web.pdf.

———. 2012. "Emerging Economies and the Emergence of South-South Protectionism." Policy Research Working Paper 6162, World Bank, Washington, DC.

Buenos Aires Delivery. 2012. "Buenos Aires espera falta masiva de sushi." March 14. http://buenosairesdelivery.com/blog_es/2012/03/%C2%BFadonde-fue-todo-el-sushi.

Clarín. 2011. "Se aceleró en Agosto la salida de capitales." September 10.

Conclave Político. 2011. "Crearon Unidad de Coordinación y Evaluación de Subsidios al Consumo Interno." February 25. http://www.conclavepolitico.com/noticias_ver.php?not_codigo=17176.

Delletorre, Raúl. 2011. "Cristina de Kirchner: Trabajo argentino hasta en el ultimo clavo." Avanzar, November 30. http://www.avanzarcolombia.com/index.php?option=com_content&view=article&id=930:cristina-de-kirchner-trabajo-argentino-hasta-en-el-ultimo-clavo&catid=1:latinoamerica&Itemid=2.

De Santis, Juan Pablo. 2011. "Denuncian por presuntas coimas a un asesor del Ministerio de Industria." *La Nación*, December 29. http://www.lanacion.com.ar/1435850-un-fiscal-federal-denuncio-presuntas-coimas-para-liberar-importaciones.

Directorate General of Statistics and Censuses. 2011. "Síntesis Estadística: Tierra del Fuego, 2010–2011." Directorate General of Statistics and Censuses, Río Grande, Argentina. http://economia.tierradelfuego.gov.ar/wp-content/uploads/2011/09/Sintesis_Estadistica_2011.pdf.

El Cronista. 2012. "Tras el consejo de la Corte, se presentaron amparos contra el corralito cambiario." June 1. http://www.cronista.com/economiapolitica/Tras-el-consejo-de-la-Corte-se-presentaron-amparos-contra-el-corralito-cambiario-20120601-0071.html.

Esteban, Nicolás. 2011. "Motos: El gobierno quiere un motor de producción nacional." Autoclase, September 26. http://www.autoclase.com.ar/wp/motos-el-gobierno-quiere-un-motor-de-produccion-nacional.

Ferrer, Aldo. 1983. *Vivir con lo nuestro*. Buenos Aires: Fondo de Cultura Económica.

Finger, J. Michael. 2012. "Flexibilities, Rules, and Trade Remedies in the GATT/WTO System." In *The Oxford Handbook on the World Trade Organization*, edited by Amrita Narlikar, Martin Daunton, and Robert M. Stern, 418–40. Oxford, U.K.: Oxford University Press.

Finger, J. Michael, and Julio J. Nogués, eds. 2006. *Safeguards and Antidumping in Latin American Trade Liberalization: Fighting Fire with Fire*. New York: Palgrave Macmillan.

Gerchunoff, Pablo, and Pablo Fajgelbaum. 2005. "Two Distant Cousins: An Essay on the Comparative Economic History of Argentina and Australia." Fundación PENT, Buenos Aires.

Hebebrand, Charlotte. 2011. "What Is the Role of Trade in Reducing Price Volatility?" Remarks at the International Food Policy Research Institute seminar titled "Informing the G-20 Agenda: Actions to Address Food Price Volatility," Washington, DC, June 14.

Infobae. 2011. "Argentina es el país del mundo que más demora el ingreso de importaciones." June 5. http://www.infobae.com/notas/585728-Argentina-es-el-pais-del-mundo-que-mas-demora-el-ingreso-de-importaciones.html.

Informe Urbano. 2010. "'La sustitución de importaciones significa más trabajo y mano de obra argentina': Mercedes Benz volve." December 20. http://informeurbano.com.ar/Noticia/3650/La-sustitucion-de-importaciones-significa-mas-trabajo-y-mano-de-obra-argentinaMercedes-Benz-volvera-a-producir-camiones-en-el-pais/.

Jacquelin, Claudio. 2012. "Moreno en su mundo perfecto." *La Nación*, March 25. http://www.lanacion.com.ar/1459139-moreno-en-su-mundo-perfecto.

Kanenguiser, Martín. 2012. "Desgastado por Moreno y con una causa penal, se fue Bianchi." *La Nación*, April 10. http://www.lanacion.com.ar/1463676-desgastado-por-moreno-y-con-una-causa-penal-se-fue-bianchi.

La Mañana de Neuquén. 2012. "Admiten que se perdieron más de 4,000 empleos por trabas a las importaciones." March 29. http://www.lmneuquen.com.ar/noticias/2012/3/27/admiten-que-se-perdieron-mas-de-4000-empleos-por-trabas-a-las-importaciones_141764.

La Nación. 2009. "El censo agropecuario confirmó la desaparición de 57,000 explotaciones." October 30.

———. 2011. "Agroquímicos: Absurda restricción." November 19. http://www.lanacion.com.ar/1424578-agroquimicos-absurda-restriccion.

———. 2012a. "'Moreno es un patriota,' dijeron en la UIA." March 29. http://www.lanacion.com.ar/1460568-moreno-es-un-patriota-dijeron-en-la-uia.

———. 2012b. "Todos los libros importados están parados." March 29. http://www.lanacion.com.ar/1460603-todos-los-libros-importados-estan-parados.

La Opinión. 2007. "El gobierno subió las retenciones a las exportaciones agrícolas." November 8.

La Voz. 2010. "China criticó la medidas antidumping de Argentina y amenaza con represalias." April 22. http://www.lavoz.com.ar/content/china-critico-la-medidas-antidumping-de-argentina-y-amenaza-con-represalias.

Llach, Juan. 2002. "La industria: 1945–1983." IAE Business School, Universidad Austral, Buenos Aires.

Longoni, Matías. 2010. "China levanta la prohibición y vuelve a comprar aceite de soja." *Clarín*, October 12. http://www.clarin.com/politica/China-levanta-prohibicion-comprar-aceite_0_352164842.html.

———. 2011. *Fuera de control*. Buenos Aires: Editorial Planeta.

Losauro, Hernán. 2011. "Cristina Fernández de Kirchner: 'Debemos profundizar la sustitución de importaciones.'" Ahora Cuyo, August 5.

Ministry of Industry. 2011a. "BMW acordó con el gobierno un plan para equilibrar su balanza comercial en 2012." Press Release, October 13. http://www.industria.gob.ar/bmw-acordo-con-el-gobierno-un-plan-para-equilibrar-su-balanza-comercial-en-2012/.

———. 2011b. "Giorgi: 'Argentina sigue garantizando la rentabilidad industrial para que los empresarios textiles profundicen la inversión e integren aún más la cadena productiva.'" Press Release, September 15. http://www.industria.gob.ar/?p=9119.

———. 2011c. "Giorgi, Boudou y Moreno suscribieron el plan de exportaciones e importaciones de General Motors. Press Release, May 2. http://www.industria.gob.ar/giorgi-boudou-y-moreno-suscribieron-el-plan-de-exportaciones-e-importaciones-de-general-motors/.

———. 2011d. "Se consolida el polo electrónico de Tierra del Fuego: Hay inversiones por US$120 millones, aumentó la producción y se generaron 2.100 puestos de trabajo." Press Release, January 10. http://www.sub-industria.gob.ar/blog/2011/01/10/se-consolida-el-polo-electronico-de-tierra-del-fuego-hay-inversiones-por-us-120-millones-aumento-la-produccion-y-se-generaron-2-100-puestos-de-trabajo/.

Moore, Michael O. 2011. "Argentina: There and Back Again." In *The Great Recession and Import Protection: The Role of Temporary Trade Barriers*, edited by Chad P. Bown, 317–50. Washington, DC: World Bank. http://www.cepr.org/pubs/books/CEPR/great_recession_web.pdf.

Nogués, Julio J. 2011a. "Agricultural Export Barriers and Domestic Prices: Argentina during the Last Decade." Paper prepared for the Food and Agriculture Organization of the United Nations, Rome, June. http://www.ucema.edu.ar/conferencias/download/2012/06.15AN.pdf.

———. 2011b. *Agro e Industria: Del Centenario al Bicentenario*. Buenos Aires: Ciudad Argentina y Hispania Libros.

Nogués, Julio J., and Elías A. Baracat. 2006. "Political Economy of Antidumping and Safeguards in Argentina." In *Safeguards and Antidumping in Latin American Trade Liberalization: Fighting Fire with Fire*, edited by J. Michael Finger and Julio J. Nogués, 45–78. New York: Palgrave Macmillan.

Nogués, Julio J., and Alberto Porto. 2007. "Evaluación de impactos económicos y sociales de políticas públicas en la cadena agroindustrial." Foro de la Cadena Agroindustrial, Buenos Aires. http://www.foroagroindustrial.org.ar/pdf/final_home_old.pdf.

Patagonia en Baires. 2011. "Ríos defendió el régimen promocional tecnológico." October 11. http://www.patagoniaenbaires.com.ar/Noticia/tierra-del-fuego/rios-defendio-el-regimen-promocional-tecnologico-11-10-2011-14-07-51.

Perry, Guillermo. 2003. "Can Fiscal Rules Help Reduce Volatility in Latin America and the Caribbean." Policy Research Working Paper 3080, World Bank, Washington, DC. http://www-wds.worldbank.org/external/default/WDSContentServer/IW3P/IB/2003/07/26/000094946_03071704235094/Rendered/PDF/multi0page.pdf.

ProChile. 2010. "Importadores vendrán a Viña del Mar al XIV Encuentro Empresarial del 12 al 14 de mayo 2010." May. http://www.prochile.cl/valparaiso/noticias.php?item=0000011064.

Sturzenegger, Adolfo C., and Mariana Salazni. 2007. "Distortions to Agricultural Incentives in Argentina." Agricultural Distortions Paper 11, World Bank, Washington, DC. http://siteresources.worldbank.org/INTTRADERESEARCH/Resources/544824-1146153362267/Argentina_1207.pdf.

Webb, Richard, Josefina Camminati, and Raúl León Thorne. 2006. "Antidumping Mechanisms and Safeguards in Peru." In *Safeguards and Antidumping in Latin American Trade Liberalization: Fighting Fire with Fire*, edited by J. Michael Finger and Julio J. Nogués, 247–77. New York: Palgrave Macmillan.

World Bank. 2010. "Enterprise Surveys: Argentina." World Bank, Washington, DC. http://espanol.enterprisesurveys.org/Data/ExploreEconomies/2010/argentina#regulations-and-taxes--sin-subgrupos.

WTO (World Trade Organization). 2007. *Trade Policy Review: Argentina, 2007.* Blue Ridge Summit, PA: Bernan Press.

———. 2011. "Committee on Import Licensing Procedures: Minutes of the Meeting held on October 14." WTO, Geneva, Switzerland. http://docsonline.wto.org/GEN_highLightParent.asp?qu=%28+%40meta%5FSymbol+G%FCLIC%FCM%FC%2A+%29+&doc=D%3A%2FDDFDOCUMENTS%2FT%2FG%2FLIC%2FM34%2EDOC%2EHTM&curdoc=3&popTitle=G%2FLIC%2FM%2F34.

CHAPTER 4

Peru and Argentina: Different Paths

Introduction

Factually, the principal finding of this study is that Peru's reforms have continued over several different presidential administrations, whereas Argentina's have been reversed. In both countries, the introduction of new mechanisms for managing trade policy had been part of the reforms. As Peru's liberalization has expanded, the new institutions have become more robust, and pressures for protection have been managed through the new mechanisms. At the same time, Argentine trade policy has returned to the highly protective import substitution regime in place before the 1990 reforms. Multiple restrictions have been imposed, mostly through a reversion to informal methods that eschew the procedural characteristics that World Trade Organization trade remedy rules advance and that the 1990 reforms attempted to introduce into Argentine governance.

In the sections that follow, we summarize the Peru and Argentina studies and bring forward key findings of each.[1] We then look into possible explanations for why reform has continued in Peru but foundered in Argentina.

Peru

Alberto Fujimori became president of Peru in 1990 within the context of one of the most severe economic and political crises in the country's history. Peru was experiencing hyperinflation. Domestic production had fallen by 20 percent in the two preceding years. Through taxation and ownership of companies, the government controlled more than half of the gross domestic product (GDP), yet government provision of education, police, sanitation, and so forth had been severely reduced because of fiscal impoverishment, corruption, and growing terrorism. The import regime included a high tariff (average rate, 66 percent) supplemented by import bans on a number of products. These elements, together with a number of tariff exemptions, created extreme positive and negative levels of effective protection.

Reform That Has Taken Root

These conditions provided an entry point for reform. During the presidential campaign of 1990, candidate Mario Vargas Llosa's liberal message was no longer regarded as a rationalization for big business and became instead a legitimate argument for the national interest. Fujimori, once elected, realized that the results of the old economic policy had been disastrous. Though he was not elected on a liberal platform, his lack of political debts, his practical way of seeing things, and his sense of public support for change led him to take the liberal path.

Congressional opposition to his proposed reforms led Fujimori to close down the Congress, a move that the Peruvian public widely supported. The public, more than the Congress, was convinced that change was necessary and that the reform program—which had been elaborated by Vargas Llosa and then taken up by Fujimori—would indeed make things better. Thus, Peru's reforms began with widespread public support, but under an autocratic government.

Economic disaster in many countries has been an entry point for reform, but in many instances, reforms have been abandoned shortly thereafter. Peru is emerging as one of the exceptions. The reforms in Peru have brought economic success, which has brought forth support for further reform. In 2001, when Alejandro Toledo was elected president, he was heavily pressed by the populace, civil organizations, business, and trade unions to select a minister of economy and a central bank chair with excellent professional reputations: people of sufficient stature who would guarantee the continuity of the ongoing reforms. Toledo's crucial decision to do so reignited the dynamic forces toward openness and competition. (One astute Peruvian observed, "Toledo had not many alternatives. It was either push the correct/publicly acclaimed green button or the disaster red button."[2]) On being elected in 2006, Alan García Pérez made a similar decision, even though in his earlier term as president he, like Toledo, had been critical of opening the Peruvian economy into the global economy.

Positive Results

The 1990–2011 reform period has been perhaps the most successful period of economic and social development in Peruvian history. During those two decades, GDP tripled, exports multiplied by 14, and international reserves multiplied by 37. Inflation has been low, averaging below 4 percent in the past decade; public external debt is only 11.4 percent of GDP today; and government income has increased from 8.1 percent to 21 percent of GDP. Social indicators show similar progress. Growth of rural capital income from 2000 to 2010 was 6.6 percent per year compared with an average of 0.7 percent from 1900 to 2000. Travel hours to the nearest city for residents of rural districts decreased from 14 in 2001 to 5 in 2011, because of improvements in the national road network. In the rural districts, daily wages doubled and house values tripled; infant mortality and extreme poverty indicators were reduced by 50 percent in the same period.[3]

Trade Policy Evolves

At the beginning of chapter 2, we reminded the reader that trade policy is only a part of comprehensive reform, albeit a critical one. Peruvian trade policy has moved from an extreme import substitution regime to an economy with minimal trade restrictions and sound discipline in the management of pressures for new protection.

Trade reform did not begin, whole cloth, with a new trade policy plan. It began, on the negative side, from the recognized need to move away from disaster of the old policy regime and, on the positive side, from the Asian example. The Asian example provided a general sense of what to do, but perhaps more important, it buoyed Peruvian self-confidence that the country could succeed as part of the global economy. Earlier attempts at economic integration had been in reality extensions of the import substitution regime. The Andean Community of Nations (Comunidad Andina de Naciones, or CAN) was a plan for a negotiated division in which members would produce products for the entire community, with guarantees against competition from outside CAN or even from other CAN producers.[4] This time, Peruvians began to believe that they could hold their own with the world.

Asian Economies as an Example

The successes of Asian countries have had a considerable influence on Peru. Some say that Fujimori's Japanese background contributed significantly to his election in 1990. As president, Fujimori paid close attention to the relationships with the Pacific Basin economies. At his initiative, the government used participation in Asia-Pacific Economic Cooperation meetings to provide Peruvian business leaders opportunities to network with Asian business leaders.

Although the Asian example was generally in the background from the beginning, in 2001, the Ministry of Economy and Finance (MEF)[5] prepared a study that compared Peru's progress with that of several Asian countries, particularly the Republic of Korea and Taiwan, China. In 1970, these countries had per capita incomes more or less equal to that of Peru. However, over the following three decades, per capita income in those countries had increased significantly more than it had in Peru. This study played a major part in the Toledo government's winning authorization from the Congress to create a trade ministry that would bring new focus and dynamism to Peru's integration into the global economy. The study demonstrated that a country starting from the position that Peru then occupied could succeed, and it received considerable attention within Peruvian civil society, as well as in the business community.

A Practical Approach

Reform leaders began with concrete steps, such as reducing tariffs and revising foreign investment laws, through which leadership hoped to augment competitiveness in the local economy and to attract foreign investment. Through such reforms, leaders hoped to support the importation of the capital goods needed to improve domestic productivity and to expand Peru's export earnings.

The details of the policy would emerge as success, experience, and knowledge accumulated. Some early but timid steps were taken toward improving access to foreign markets, but only in 2001 would negotiations with other countries become an active part of the emerging strategy.

INDECOPI and the Professionalization of Management of Pressures for Protection

An important part of trade policy reform was the installation of trade remedies (safeguards, antidumping, countervailing duties) sanctioned by the General Agreement on Tariffs and Trade (GATT) and World Trade Organization (WTO) as the mechanisms through which the government would formalize management of domestic pressures for protection. Effective administration of the new laws and procedures would require more than technical expertise, it would also require independence from political power. Moreover, the culture of decision making (the mindset of the responsible officials) would have to change: from one in which decisions were based on long-standing relationships to one in which decisions were based on the facts of economic potential.

To this end, the government (in 1992, when Fujimori was president) created by law the National Institute for the Defense of Competition and the Protection of Intellectual Property (Instituto Nacional de Defensa de la Competencia y de la Protección de la Propiedad Intelectual, or INDECOPI). INDECOPI's overall responsibility is to maintain a competitive market economy in Peru. Organizationally, it is a collection of autonomous commissions that provide the functional and regulatory frameworks for competition policy, intellectual property, small business development, and other parts of the infrastructure of a market economy. One of the commissions, the Antidumping and Countervailing Measures Commission, is responsible for antidumping and countervailing duty investigations and for the imposition of measures. This commission is also the investigating authority for safeguard cases, the final decision on such cases being made by a multisector commission formed by several ministers.[6]

Peru has been one of the world's most successful countries at confining protectionist pressures within formal trade remedy mechanisms and in maintaining discipline over new restrictions. During the current recession, Peru has imposed few trade controls (see table 4.1), and those that have been imposed have been INDECOPI-administered antidumping or countervailing measures.

Trade Agreements Enter the Arsenal of Policy Management

By the turn of the millennium, the vision of Peru as a successful part of the world economy had spread nationally; that is why Toledo chose to proceed as he did. This view and the accumulating success and confidence laid the base for reform leaders to recognize and seize another opportunity.

The U.S. Andean Trade Preference Act (ATPA) provided a positive spark to Peru's vision of itself in the world economy. This law, passed by the U.S. Congress in 1991, provided for reduced tariffs on imports from Peru and other Andean countries in exchange for their cooperation in the war against drugs. As such,

Table 4.1 Trade Control Measures Reported by Global Trade Alert, 2008–11, by Formal or Informal Process for Application and Administration

	Share of import control measures (%)		*Number of measures*			
Country	*Formal process*	*Informal process*	*Import control measures, formal and informal*	*Export support measures*	*Export restriction measures*	*Support measures for domestic production*
Argentina	40	60	108	1	7	10
Indonesia	40	60	20	0	5	7
Ukraine	56	44	9	0	2	3
Thailand	60	40	5	1	1	0
Japan	64	36	11	8	1	7
China	67	33	46	7	10	11
United States	76	24	17	2	0	13
Mexico	85	15	13	0	0	0
Russian Federation	85	15	68	3	13	61
India	86	14	50	13	10	2
South Africa	90	10	20	0	0	4
Brazil	91	9	46	8	1	6
European Union	94	6	32	4	1	1
Turkey	100	0	11	0	0	1
Vietnam	100	0	8	1	3	0
Peru	100	0	7	0	0	0
Australia	100	0	6	0	0	7
Korea, Rep.	100	0	5	9	0	5

Source: Data from Global Trade Alert, "Implementing Country and Measure Type" (http://www.globaltradealert.org/data-exports).
Note: Countries listed are those with five or more import control measures listed in the source table. They are ranked by percentage of measures by informal process. Data included are for implemented measures that are coded *restrictive. Formal* in this tabulation includes trade defense measures and tariff measures; *informal* includes nontariff measures that are not otherwise specified, technical barriers to trade, sanitary and phytosanitary measures, import quotas, and import bans. *Support measures for domestic production* includes bailout or state aid measures, public procurement, local content requirement, and support for state-controlled companies. *Export support measures* include export subsidies and support for export financing. *Export restriction measures* include export taxes and quantitative restrictions on exports.

ATPA demanded minimal change in Peru's trade policies, but it provided an opportunity for Peruvian companies to do business in the United States.

The creation of the ATPA program caused the Peruvian government to see the potential for something more. The need, however, to renew the agreement every three years and its initial exclusion of labor-intensive industries such as textiles lessened the program's usefulness as an incentive for investment in the export sector. Having been made aware of the immense U.S. market and having sampled success in that market, Peruvian officials decided that when the ATPA came up for renewal in 2001, they would seek a more ambitious agreement. The United States first saw Peru as a partner in the war against drugs; Peruvian leaders would exploit this view to create for itself a role as economic partner.

Double Strategy with Double Objectives

Government leaders recognized that they would not succeed in such a purpose without the participation and conviction of the business community and civil society. As they moved toward negotiation of a trade agreement with the United States, they prepared a dual agenda, one for the external front and one for the domestic front. The agendas would share several objectives: (a) to make the Peruvian economy more productive; (b) to build up the image of Peru and Peruvians as members of the international community, which would put Peru and Peruvians on the world's economic and political radar; and (c) to expand the confidence of Peruvians that they belonged there.

The government was diligent in enlisting the participation of all sectors of Peruvian society; it organized more than 600 events with business associations, labor unions, chambers of commerce, universities, professional associations, agricultural communities, and fishermen, among others. Continuing input was organized through 21 advisory groups, one for each of the areas of negotiation.

A New Government Ministry Oriented toward Integration into the World Economy

The ATPA negotiations provided an opportunity for reform leaders to press for a major change within the government: to create the Ministry of Foreign Commerce and Tourism (Ministerio de Comercio Exterior y Turismo, or MINCETUR) to replace the Ministry of Industry, Tourism, and Commercial Negotiations. This change allowed the creation of a unit focused on negotiations with the United States and, later, on negotiations with other countries. Of perhaps even greater importance, the change facilitated a reorientation of trade policy toward Peruvian companies that were enthusiastic about participating in the modern international economy. The previous ministry had been oriented toward Peruvian businesses that were more concerned with avoiding exposure to international competition.

Role of Free Trade Agreement Negotiations in Forming Peruvian Trade Policy

Since completing the free trade agreement (FTA) with the United States in April 2005, Peru has also negotiated and signed agreements with Canada, Chile, China, Costa Rica, the European Free Trade Association, the European Union (EU), Japan, Korea, Panama, Singapore, and Thailand.

Without belittling the value of these negotiations for building commercial relationships, chapter 2 reveals that their role has been much more. For one thing, the negotiations have been a vehicle through which successive governments have kept before the Peruvian public the benefits of integration into the world economy. President Alan García often used the slogan *montarse a la ola del crecimiento* (ride the wave of growth) to rally Peruvians to the spirit of attracting investment from and competing in the markets of the strongest economies in the world (García Pérez 2011).

Targeting specific and prominent countries has provided identity for the new vision that participation in WTO negotiations could not provide. The FTA negotiations have allowed Peru to establish its own identity among trading nations; they have allowed Peru to set its own pace of liberalization; and they have raised in the public mind the idea that Peruvian leaders can be shapers of the accords. Large countries such as Brazil, India, and the United States can use their participation in WTO negotiations as part of their management of the domestic politics of trade policy, but there is simply not enough room on the multilateral stage for Peruvian officials to do the same.

The Momentum of the FTA Carries beyond Its Requirements

No less important, reform leaders used the positive image created by the negotiations to move reform beyond the demands of the agreement. Before the Peru-U.S. FTA was approved in the United States, elections there had shifted political control, and the U.S. Congress insisted on renegotiating some aspects of the FTA. Had the executive branch of the Peruvian government been tepid in its support for the new trade philosophy, it might have seen this renegotiation as an opportunity to slow the liberalization process in Peru. It chose the opposite course. Between March and June 2008, the government submitted more than 100 supreme decrees to the Congress for approval. These decrees included not only the subjects required to meet the terms of the FTA negotiation, but also other subjects that constituted a kind of second-generation reform, in an effort to prepare and adapt to Peru's participation in the global market.

Peru's endemic approach to liberalization would be expanded in 2005 by an MEF resolution, discussed next.

A Policy Blueprint Emerges

The story of Peruvian trade reform began with the rejection of policies that had obviously failed and the confidence that Peru could achieve what a number of Asian countries had achieved. The reform developed concrete elements as policy entrepreneurs created and expanded opportunities.

In time, the government put together a blueprint for reform that built on the various threads that had emerged. In 2005, MEF approved a ministry resolution titled *Tariff Policy Guidelines* that outlined in broad scope the country's development policy, with particular focus on policies related to integration into the world economy (MEF 2005). With respect to tariff policy, the resolution provides a rationale for unilateral liberalization. It takes up the tariff as a tax imposed only on imported goods, thereby imparting a protective bias. It goes on to recommend that policy management maintain a balance among the tariff's impacts on output, employment, revenue and efficiency in resource allocation.

> From a standpoint of economic efficiency, the reduction of tariffs promotes improvements in international competitiveness, productivity of businesses, and improvements of domestically produced products. All of this enables higher incomes and greater customer satisfaction. Higher tariffs isolate an economy from international competition and provide only a few sectors a boost at the expense of the economy's overall efficiency.
>
> Hence policy, particularly for a country with no power to influence international prices, should be to reduce tariffs and thereby their distorting effect on the efficiency of resource allocation. Resource allocation should be by market criteria rather than by the creation of artificial advantages.

> This argument is equally valid against congressional bills that seek to promote sectors through tariff exemptions. (MEF 2005, 67–68)

This resolution has remained the basic document of international trade policies through the two changes of government that have occurred since it was first promulgated.

Inclusion

Reform leaders have been diligent in enlisting the participation of all sectors of Peruvian society. As noted earlier, as part of the negotiation of the FTA with the United States, the government organized more than 600 events with various sectors and continued to gather input through 21 standing advisory groups.

Reform leaders with whom we spoke emphasized that in those meetings and other contacts, they put great emphasis on hearing what the business community had to say and including it in government activities and in all negotiations. This approach, they explained, was also part of the Asian example.

Change Is a Cumulative Process

> *Long-run economic change is the cumulative consequence of innumerable short-run decisions by political and economic entrepreneurs.*
>
> —Douglass C. North (1990, 104)

In the case of Peru, the institutions and the individuals responsible for developing policy have been receptive to good economics and have responded to it. Peru's example shows that increased economic prosperity is not a one-time change to a different set of policy parameters. It is the cumulative consequence of many decisions guided by an ensemble of examples, objectives, and values that bring better economics into the institutional structure of the economy—each of these decisions supported by the confidence that the overall program will succeed.

Argentina

The Argentina study documents the extensive restrictions imposed, the reversion to informal methods for managing trade policy, and the lack of effective resistance either from domestic interests that bear the costs of trade restrictions or from the international community. Except for a brief period of liberalization in the 1990s, Argentina has been a relatively closed economy over the past eight decades. During that period, the Argentine economy has performed poorly compared with those of countries with similar resources that have adopted open policies. In 1930, Argentina's per capita income was approximately 85 percent of Australia's. But since Australia shifted to an open trade strategy, the ratio has fallen to 30 percent. Moreover, Argentina's protectionist regime has not provided a redistribution of income toward workers. Since 1960, the ratio of wages to GDP per worker has remained constant in Australia, but it has fallen by some 40 percent in Argentina.

In the 1990s, the government in power sought to implement an open competitive market with marked reduction of government intervention (Nogués and Baracat 2006). Major sectors of the economy that were dominated by public enterprises were privatized, and foreign investment was put on an equal footing with domestic investment. Tariff rates that had averaged 40 percent in the mid-1980s fell to an average of 14 percent by the mid-1990s. On imports from MERCOSUR partners, most rates fell to zero. This liberalization was accompanied by the introduction of disciplined mechanisms for managing pressures for protection: GATT/WTO-sanctioned antidumping and safeguard mechanisms.

However, this liberalization was short-lived, and starting with the *corralito*[7] in late 2001, the governments in power since then have reversed it. The past decade has seen reversion to the policy profile that has dominated in previous decades:

- The return to an import substitution strategy was announced.
- The country reverted to instruments of trade control that lack the transparency and accountability that the WTO system attempts to foster. The procedural and governance regulations introduced in the 1990s have been displaced by nontransparent and discretionally implemented restriction mechanisms.
- Widespread import controls were implemented. Ultimately (early 2012), as the peso became increasingly overvalued, government approval was required for each request to purchase foreign exchange.
- Export-balancing or countertrade requirements became a condition for importing.
- Quantitative export restrictions and high export taxes were placed on cereal and bovine meat exports.
- Targeted industry support measures were implemented.

Return to Import Substitution

The Argentine government has publicly acknowledged a return to an import substitution trade strategy, which is reinforced by limiting imports in many sectors to the value of exports of the sector. Box 4.1 provides a summary timeline of government documents and statements from ministers and from the president, to this effect.

The new import substitution rationale repeats much of the rhetoric of the past. It ensures that domestic producers so supported will also compete well in export markets. Protecting domestic employment is the major political rationale; it emphasizes the necessity to deal with "unfair" foreign competition, which usually refers to imports from Asia.

Return to Informal Governance of Trade Controls

Table 4.1 reports the Global Trade Alert tabulation of trade restrictions and trade-affecting industry support measures. Global Trade Alert, a project supported by the World Bank and other organizations, is motivated by the concern that the Great Recession could bring a resurgence of trade restrictions. In addition to including all measures for which the WTO agreements require

Box 4.1 Progression of Import Substitution Policy in Argentina

Table B4.1 documents the building of the new Argentine protectionism by citing specific events and statements by government officials and informed observers. Although events have accelerated since 2007, an ideology that does not oppose any demand for protection was already apparent in 2003.

Table B4.1 Import Substitution Policy Timeline

Date	*Authorities' declarations*
December 23, 2003	Resolution 220/2003-SICPME initiated the system on import licensing for bicycles. This event was more or less the commencement of Argentina's new protectionism. The resolution also created the administrative procedures for enforcing the restrictions. *Source:* InfoLEG database website at http://infoleg.mecon.gov.ar/infolegInternet/anexos/90000-94999/91398/norma.htm.
August 11, 2005	Argentina limits entry points for certain goods. By virtue of General Resolution 1924 of August 11, 2005, and with the purpose of strengthening customs controls, the Federal Public Revenue Administration limited the points of entry for certain categories of goods, including textiles, shoes and toys. On January 29, 2010, the General Customs Division passed new legislation, adding several new tariff positions to the regime. (Only tariff positions added in this new legislation have been included in this reported measure.) *Source:* Global Trade Alert 2010b.
August 17, 2007	President Cristina Fernández de Kirchner and Minister of Economy Miguel Peirano announced measures to restrict imports, especially those from East Asia. The restrictions covered textiles, footwear, toys, leather goods, and computers. The measures applied included minimum values to collect duties, specialized customs offices designation for certain products, new technical standards for certain products, expansion of the coverage of the import licensing system, and increased customs checks on products originating in certain Asian countries. Shortly thereafter, China announced that it was considering retaliation measures on oil soy. *Sources: ADN Mundo* 2007; iProfessional.com 2007.
November 2, 2009	Law 26,457, enacted on December 10, 2008, created an incentive scheme for local investment in manufacturing motorcycles and motorcycle parts. The scheme includes new restrictions on imports of assembled vehicles and a tax deduction based on purchases of parts from local manufacturers. Débora Giorgi, the minister of industry and tourism, while speaking before the Association of Motorcycle Manufacturers, announced that to promote import substitution the law would encourage domestic production of motorcycles and motorcycle parts, the expectation being that within five years imported parts would constitute no more than 30 percent of the production value of a unit. *Sources: Ámbito Financiero* at http://190.224.163.233/ambitoweb/diario/2009/1126/texto/Not_20091126_495325.rtf; Río Negro 2012.

table continues next page

box continues next page

Box 4.1 Progression of Import Substitution Policy in Argentina *(continued)*

Table B4.1 Import Substitution Policy Timeline *(continued)*

Date	*Authorities' declarations*
November 3, 2009	Law 26,393, enacted on June 25, 2008, created a system of bonuses payable to assemblers of vehicles, internal combustion engines, gearboxes, and axles that purchase locally made parts. *Source:* Honorable Chamber of Deputies website at http://www.hcdn.gov.ar/leyes/buscarNormasXNumLey.jsp?id_norma=40118.
February 5, 2010	On February 5, 2010, the government passed implementing legislation that put into effect the Local Investment Incentives Regime for Motorcycles and Motorcycle Parts Manufacturing, originally established in 2009 by Law 26,457 and Decree 1857/2009. Under the regime, local producers of motorcycles and certain motorcycle parts will receive two types of benefits: (a) reductions of duties levied on imported inputs, ranging from 20 to 60 percent of current import duty rates, and (b) tax credits on purchases of locally produced inputs. To be eligible for the benefits, applicants have to pledge investments of at least US$1 million in real estate, facilities, machinery, and development of local suppliers. Furthermore, to continue to be eligible for the benefit, they have to gradually reduce the foreign content of their output, with a view of reaching a 30 percent ceiling in foreign content by 2015. *Source:* Global Trade Alert 2010a.
May 2010	At the 15th Trans-Andes Encuentro Empresarial, a Chilean spokesperson commented that while Argentina is a large market for food, Argentine government policies have been creating difficulties regarding the sale of imported food items. Managers of supermarket chains, supermarkets, and other retail stores have received verbal communication from the secretary of commerce that they should stop importing, among other items, canned corn and tomatoes from Brazil, Swiss chocolates, Greek peaches, and nuts and other Chilean products that are processed in the local market. The secretary of commerce has instructed the National Food Institute, which formerly issued certificates of free movement of goods, to redirect all requests for such certificates to the Secretariat of Commerce. *Source:* Boeninger 2010.
January 21, 2011	In a presentation announcing the regime for promotion of modems and tablets in Tierra del Fuego, Débora Giorgi, the minister of industry, stated, "Companies' interest in manufacturing in Tierra del Fuego clearly indicates that we are on the path to a national electronics industry. We will continue to promote this strategic sector. We aim to replace imports of high-technology goods and generate new jobs." *Source:* Ministry of Industry 2011a.
February 22, 2011	Débora Giorgi, the minister of industry, said that "the changing economic and political paradigm that began in 2003 continues to ensure historical rates of growth with social inclusion." She reiterated the importance of continuing to preserve the domestic market for domestic production. "The import substitution we are encouraging is a cornerstone for the growth of our economy … so we have extended the list of products on which import licensing is applied." *Source:* Ministry of Industry 2011c.

table continues next page

box continues next page

Box 4.1 Progression of Import Substitution Policy in Argentina *(continued)*

Table B4.1 Import Substitution Policy Timeline *(continued)*

Date	*Authorities' declarations*
February 25, 2011	The ministers of economy and industry met with 300 entrepreneurs from all sectors of the country, noting that the government "applies trade administration as a way to guide import substitution and generate more production and jobs in Argentina." They urged sectors that import products covered by the import licensing system to invest in job creation in Argentina, pointing out that the sectors would be monitored as to the quantity, the quality, and the prices of the products they supplied to the Argentine market. *Source:* Ministry of Industry 2011b.
March 10, 2011	The Ministry of Industry announced that imports of cars and inputs used by local car producers will be limited to the value of local production that they export. The restriction is aimed at reducing the increasing trade deficit in the sector. Imports originating in MERCOSUR and Mexico will be exempt from the restriction. The measure was announced during a meeting of government officers with top representatives of the automotive industry and will not be laid down in any regulation or written instrument other than the meeting's press release. To obtain the necessary import permits, car producers will have to submit a sworn statement in which they set forth their exports plans and get the approval of the Ministry of Industry. By April 2011, most car producers, including Volkswagen, Mercedes-Benz, Porsche, PSA Peugeot-Citröen, and Alfa Romeo had concluded agreements with the government in which they committed to reduce their trade deficits by balancing exports and imports. Firms that do not have local car production undertook to export goods other than cars or auto parts. Such was the case of Alfa Romeo and Porsche, which pledged to export biofuel and wines, respectively. *Source:* Global Trade Alert 2011a.
May 3, 2011	On March 10, 2011, the Ministry of Industry adopted a verbal measure whereby imports of cars and inputs used by local car producers would be limited to the value of local production that they export. Starting on May 3, 2011, local media reported that similar restrictions were being extended to the pharmaceutical industry. As in the case of the automotive industry, local suppliers of pharmaceutical products were required to submit deficit reduction plans as a condition to obtaining the necessary import permits. To prevent supply shortages in the local market, only locally produced medicines are subject to the measure. *Source:* Global Trade Alert 2011b.
June 22, 2011	In opening the forum for the value chain of textiles and apparel (part of Argentina's Strategic Plan 2020), Débora Giorgi, the minister of industry, declared that "we will continue to have a strong domestic market, protected against unfair competition." She elaborated that restrictions to dampen imports have boosted local textile production, and the challenge now is to support higher investment to further increased local production and reduction of the sectoral trade deficit. *Source:* Secretariat of Public Communication 2011.

table continues next page

box continues next page

Box 4.1 Progression of Import Substitution Policy in Argentina *(continued)*

Table B4.1 Import Substitution Policy Timeline *(continued)*

Date	*Authorities' declarations*
July 30, 2011	On March 10, 2011, the government started to adopt a series of verbal measures aimed at balancing imports and exports in certain sectors of the economy. Importers in these designated sectors are required to export an amount of local production equal to the value they import. The policy was first applied to car producers and was then extended to the pharmaceutical industry. By the end of July 2011, media reported that similar restrictions were also applied to refrigerators, washing machines, cookers, and toys. *Source:* Global Trade Alert 2011c.
November 29, 2011	"Not one nail imported, if possible," said President Cristina Fernández de Kirchner, addressing the Chamber of Construction. She stressed the need to strengthen import substitution and to lower input costs so as to improve the trade balance and create more employment in the country. Speaking to *Ultimas Noticias*, Gabriel Murara, the vice president of the Confederation of Industry of Uruguay, which is a member country of MERCOSUR, admitted concerns about this statement, adding that he saw no quick exit from problems with Argentina. *Source:* Delletore 2011.
March 22, 2012	Débora Giorgi, the minister of industry, warned agricultural machinery manufacturers that to do business in the Argentine market that they must incorporate more parts produced in Argentina. "The policy is one of carrot and stick; companies that use domestic demand must generate Argentine employment." Giorgi set a target of 50 percent local value added for the industry, and wants to see the sector reverse the trade deficit of Arg$450 million recorded in 2010. Companies such as Fiat, Case New Holland, John Deere, Pauny-Stara, Agco, and Claas have signed agreements with the government to adapt to the new policy of import substitution and countertrade. *Sources:* Infocampo 2012; Ministry of Industry 2012.

notification, Global Trade Alert covers other measures (some tailored perhaps to elude WTO restrictions) that are reported by news media as well as by importers and exporters.[8]

Table 4.1 documents not only that Argentina has applied a number of trade control measures but also that the procedural reforms of the 1990s, to a large extent, have been put aside. Sixty percent of the import controls by Argentina have been measures that Global Trade Alert classifies as "nontariff barriers (not otherwise specified)" and other measures not established through formal procedures. Moreover, procedures for antidumping and safeguards—classified in the table as "formal"—have been made less inclusive of stakeholders; for example, public hearings have been eliminated from the proceedings through which the National Commission on Foreign Trade conducts these investigations.

As chapter 3 elaborates, the import restrictions applied have taken many forms: (a) unexplained delays in release from customs, (b) additional documentation and process requirements, (c) nonresponses and delayed responses to requests for nonautomatic licenses, (d) lack of transparency in the process through which decisions are made, (e) control of technical regulations, and (f) volatility in the application of standards. For example, in September 2011, several Argentine publishers were unable to obtain the release of almost 2 million books from customs. Many of those books had been written and edited in Argentina but were shipped outside the country for printing. In separate meetings with government officials, each publishing company was told to provide a plan on how it would have its printing done in Argentina in the future and how it would change its product lines when specialized printing was unavailable domestically.

A common element in the actions reported is that the eventual release of imports depended on reaching an agreement with the government on commitments to countertrade, to substitute future domestic products for previously imported ones, and sometimes to invest in domestic facilities.

Import Licenses as Import Restrictions

To the extent that an import control has a legal form—beyond, say, shipments simply not being cleared from customs houses—it is a requirement for an import license. Such a requirement could mean, for example, that unless the BMW dealership in Argentina documents its arrangements to promote the sale of Argentine rice and leather around the world, it will not receive the necessary license to clear a shipment of imported vehicles.

According to the WTO agreement on import licensing, such systems are allowed as a means "to administer measures such as those adopted pursuant to the relevant provisions of GATT 1994"—that is, when there is some other provision in the rules that allows the import control that the license administers, such as an antidumping order. Of course, the antidumping order—to be legal within the GATT/WTO system—must satisfy the procedural and substantive requirements of GATT article VI and of the WTO agreement on antidumping.

In practice in Argentina, an import license has itself become an instrument of trade control. The demands of a trade remedy process—a criteria-based, transparent determination with stakeholders' participation—have been circumvented.

Industry Support at High Cost

This summary contains one example of the support the Argentine government has provided for selected industries or regions: the incentives for the assembly of certain electronic products in the southernmost province of Argentina, the island of Tierra del Fuego. Assemblers on Tierra del Fuego are exempt from tariffs on inputs and taxes on production that are applied on the mainland. (Protection against imports of assembled telephones includes a requirement that each visitor entering Argentina identify his or her cellular telephone, by brand and model, on the customs entry form.) Following the creation of these incentives in late 2009, the assembly of cellular phones on the island jumped from 400,000 units to 4.9 million in 2010.

As to the effects of these incentives, manufacturing jobs on Tierra del Fuego increased by approximately 2,800 in 2010, at a cost we estimate at US$230,000 per job per year. The program has not brought new technology to Argentina. To qualify for the tax exemptions, a company must produce the user's manual and the warranty card for the product locally, along with packaging and labeling materials.[9]

Export Restrictions

During the past decade, Argentina implemented widespread export taxes. These rates reached a peak around mid-2008 and are still high for major cereal products: 23 percent for wheat, 20 percent for corn, and 35 percent for soybeans. Starting in early 2006, these barriers were reinforced with quantitative restrictions on exports of wheat, corn, and bovine meat. The restrictions on exports have brought about a significant shift of cropland from cattle, wheat, and corn to soybean cultivation because soybean exports are not subject to quantitative restrictions.

These restrictions, like the import restrictions, have been administered through informal procedures. But in this case, questions about administration prompted some members of the lower house of Congress to propose the creation of a special investigation commission to look into possible irregularities in the administrative office responsible for allocating export quotas and distributing food subsidies to processors.

Export taxes are variable—for example, they are higher on wheat than on flour or bread. Hence, farm-gate prices have declined by more than food prices, suggesting that the rents created by the export restrictions have been in significant part captured by processors.

Domestic Political Support

More by default than by public debate, domestic politics have generally supported the restrictive measures. The government lost its majority in the lower chamber in the 2009 midterm elections but retained control of the Senate. In October 2011, Cristina Fernández de Kirchner was reelected president with 54 percent of the popular vote, and her party also regained majority in both houses of Congress. Import barriers and, more generally, the degree of openness of the economy were never issues in the elections; the one candidate who spoke openly of eliminating export barriers received less than 2 percent of the vote.

WTO Discipline

Several WTO members have raised questions in the Committee on Import Licensing about the possibility that the licensing procedures constituted de facto quantitative restrictions. Members have also requested information about the basis in Argentine law for the practices. On March 30, 2012, 14 WTO members (the EU being one) delivered a joint statement on Argentine restrictions at a meeting of the WTO Council for Trade in Goods. The members' statement calls on Argentina to "provide a detailed written explanation of why in its view these measures and practices are consistent with WTO rules." Argentina responded that it has "a system of automatic and nonautomatic licensing, which is compatible with WTO rules" and that the statement was intended to make Argentina "an example to discourage developing countries from using the public policies we are fairly entitled to use." The statement and Argentina's response are summarized in box 4.2.

On May 25, 2012, the EU requested consultations with Argentina under the WTO Dispute Settlement Understanding. The EU charged that Argentine measures violate GATT/WTO rules in four ways:

- Licenses labeled "automatic" are used in a nonautomatic manner.
- Licenses labeled "nonautomatic" are not covered under any allowance for restriction and are therefore prohibited quantitative restrictions.
- Nonautomatic licenses are issued in a discretionary way, through burdensome, overly long, and nontransparent procedures.
- In February 2012, Argentina introduced a preapproval requirement covering all imports.

Under the procedures of the Dispute Settlement Understanding, if the parties fail to reach a satisfactory solution within 60 days, the EU can pursue the dispute by requesting the establishment of a WTO panel that would rule on the legality of Argentina's measures.[10]

Argentina began issuing nonautomatic licenses, the main instrument of the dispute, in 2003; thus, nine years of growing dissatisfaction by members elapsed before a formal complaint was made the WTO.

Retaliation

Chapter 3 reports two instances of tit-for-tat retaliation against Argentina's trade restrictions: by China and by Brazil. In March 2012, the United States suspended Argentina's status as a beneficiary country of the Generalized System of Preferences. The U.S. announcement indicated that the reason was an investment dispute rather than a trade dispute.

Reversion to the Old Policy Culture

Argentina has reverted to inward-looking policies, most of which are administered by institutional arrangements characterized more by discretion and top-down decisions than by participatory, transparent, and accountable processes. In addition, the severity of the exchange control restrictions has intensified. The domestic currency is increasingly overvalued, and the gap between the official and black market rates is widening. Again, the exchange rate (controlled by the Central Bank) is used primarily as an instrument for controlling inflation and is not allowed to keep up with the rate of domestic inflation. Trade control measures have then a double motivation: to defend the (nominal) exchange rate and to accommodate import-competing interests. These measures are in essence the institutional arrangements and policies that characterized the protectionist era of

Box 4.2 Summaries of a Statement from 14 WTO Members Concerning Argentina's Policies and Practices Restricting Imports and of Argentina's Response

A statement was delivered on March 30, 2012, by the United States on behalf of 14 delegations, those of Australia; the European Union; Israel; Japan; the Republic of Korea; Mexico; New Zealand; Norway; Panama; Switzerland; Taiwan, China; Thailand; Turkey; and the United States.[a]

The Statement

The statement expresses concerns regarding "the nature and application of trade-restrictive measures taken by Argentina," including "the overly broad use of non-automatic import licensing trade balancing requirements, and pre-registration and pre-approval of all imports into Argentina."

The statement raises two issues about Argentina's import licensing:

- With regard to the WTO's allowing an import licensing system as being necessary only to implement an otherwise GATT/WTO legal restriction, the Argentine government has not provided such underlying rationale.
- The WTO procedural requirements for administration of licensing (for example, transparency and time limits) have not been fulfilled.

The statement goes on to note that beyond the products for which the Argentine government has announced that import licenses are necessary, the government has put in place a system requiring preregistration, review, and approval of every import transaction and that this system includes "an informal 'trade balancing' policy, whereby companies seeking to import products must agree to export, dollar for dollar, goods of an equal or greater value or establish production facilities in Argentina."

The existence of this policy is evidenced, according to the statement, by Ministry of Industry press releases announcing such trade-balancing and domestic production arrangements and by telephone calls from Argentine government officials informing importers that they must agree to undertake such trade-balancing commitments before receiving authorization to import goods.

Argentina's Response

Argentina's response (G/C/W/668, April 13, 2012) rejects the statement as having no basis in fact, as a political action (in that it does not involve precise questions concerning specific measures or policies) that seeks to pressure Argentina to revise legitimate ongoing policies. Argentina expresses concern that the statement raises systemic questions for the WTO in that it might be perceived as an unjust mechanism through which powerful members can arbitrarily censure other members with less economic clout.

The response reviews recent reforms to import procedures, insisting that "Argentina's trade policy measures are fully consistent with the international commitments it has assumed."

box continues next page

Box 4.2 Summaries of a Statement from 14 WTO Members Concerning Argentina's Policies and Practices Restricting Imports and of Argentina's Response *(continued)*

The response states that it is unfair to characterize Argentina's policies as being import restricting for two reasons:

- Such a statement prejudges their consistency with GATT/WTO rules.
- Argentina's imports have increased rapidly—recording a higher percentage increase in 2011 than any other Group of 20 country—and by 25 percent from the 14 members who signed the statement.

The response continues with a reminder of the lack of progress in the Doha Round on agriculture and the proliferation of sanitary, phytosanitary, and technical barriers and of other barriers "allegedly justified, *inter alia*, by environmental protection, animal welfare, private standards, and consumer rights."

Argentina, the response concludes, has contributed disproportionately to its size to world trade and growth. "We object, therefore, to being made into an example to discourage developing countries from using the public policies we are fairly entitled to use."

a. The statement was released on April 4, 2012, as WTO Document G/C/W/667.

Argentina's economic history. These institutions and policies are the main reason for the relative economic decline of that period.

Accounting for the Difference

The fault, dear Brutus, is not in our stars, but in ourselves.

—William Shakespeare, *Julius Caesar*, Act 1, Scene 2, lines 140–41.

Argentine governments in this decade have chosen bad trade policies. By the standards of classical economics, these policies are an inefficient and costly way to achieve the redistribution of income by which they might be rationalized. By the institutional standards exposited by Acemoglu and Robinson (2012), they are extractive and are, therefore, unlikely to promote long-term prosperity. They are a return to the policies and the processes that have been in place over the lengthy period during which Argentina's economic performance has lagged the performances of countries that have chosen less restrictive trade policies.

Peruvian governments have chosen good trade policies. By the standards of classical economics, those policies position Peruvian producers to take advantage of dynamic world markets. They also subject Peruvian producers to the discipline of international competition. Peru is building institutions that shape trade policy through transparent processes that include participation by interested parties. By Acemoglu and Robinson's (2012) standards, they are inclusive institutions and will support long-term economic growth.

Training in modern economics conditions one to look for the parameters that explain why Peru's reforms have gone in one direction and Argentina's in another. Too much can be made of such. The difference between the two experiences lies not in economic parameters such as geography or factor proportions, nor does it lie in the intensity of the economic disasters self-induced by the countries' own policies or in the severity of the external shocks they have suffered. The difference is in dominant part a matter of choice.

Institutional economics suggests that explaining such differences of choices be taken up at the level of cognitive frame—what Nobel Laureate Oliver Williamson (2000) describes as level 1 of social structure.[11] (In his schema, it is two levels above what we might call traditional or textbook economics.)

Contrary to the simple idea that thinking proceeds by discarding ideas that conflict with evidence, researchers who work in this area have found that when a person receives information that does not fit the existing frame, the information, having no place to stick, will be discounted and the frame will stay in place.[12]

If the truth does not fit the existing frame, the frame will stay in place and the truth will dissipate. It takes time and much repetition for frames to become entrenched in the very synapses of people's brains. Moreover, they have to fit together in an overall coherent way for them to make sense (Lakoff 2006, 5).

Examined at the level of frame, or spirit, Peru's reforms display a buoyant and confident attitude toward the global economy. In the words of former president Alan García, the reforms display an eagerness to "ride the wave of growth" and a confidence to "ride the tiger"—that is, to deal with the United States in the legalistic terms that characterize U.S. dealings on international trade and to come out the better for it.[13]

In comparison, Argentine trade policy continues to be made in the dependency cognitive frame long associated with that country.[14] Within that frame, interaction between Argentine buyers or sellers and the international economy will be detrimental to Argentina's interests unless that interaction is guided by government intervention. Consistent with this frame, the Argentine response to WTO members' questions about Argentina's trade policies interprets those questions as an unjust mechanism through which powerful members can arbitrarily censure other members with less economic clout (box 4.2).

In the past decade, however, the government has moved away from the reforms of trade policy governance that were introduced in the 1990s—for example, decisions made with reference to published standards, participation by interested parties, publication of policy decisions, and reasons for decisions.

Hence, a valuable part of the Peruvian example is how reform leaders put Peru's place and potential in the international economy into a new conceptual frame—particularly how they disseminated the new way of conceptualizing the relationship between Peru and the world economy among the Peruvian people, business leaders, and political leaders who have presided over the reforms.

Notes

1. These summaries should be interpreted as an invitation to read the country chapters rather than as a substitute for reading them. Certainly lessons can be drawn from these experiences in addition to those we have brought forth.
2. Quotation is from an anonymous interview.
3. Chapter 2 gives details and sources.
4. The plan had been minimally implemented.
5. In Peru, the MEF is responsible for developing the overall objectives of economic policy and for guiding the execution of those policies.
6. Webb, Camminati, and León Thorne (2006) provide a description of INDECOPI's structure and functioning, as well as of antidumping and safeguard procedures.
7. The term *corralito* refers to emergency measures put in place near the end of 2001 to stop a bank run. The government severely limited withdrawals from Argentine peso accounts and completely prohibited withdrawals from U.S. dollar–denominated accounts.
8. Here, the contribution of investigative journalism in trade liberalization has likely been underappreciated. Analyses of Australian liberalization often cite information brought forward by journalists, but we have found only one attempt to analyze the role such journalists played (McCarthy 2000).
9. Costs of this order to create jobs through trade protection are not unusual. Hufbauer and Lowry (2012) estimate, for example, that the U.S. application of additional tariffs on imports of automobile and truck tires from China saved perhaps 1,200 jobs at a cost of US$900,000 per year per job.
10. The WTO dispute settlement web page reports two other cases since 2001 in which Argentina is the respondent. Both involve formal measures: antidumping in one case and countervailing measures in the other. See the WTO's website at http://www.wto.org/english/tratop_e/dispu_e/dispu_status_e.htm.
11. A *frame* refers to a conceptual structure involved with thinking. As a part of machine translation, identifying the frame inside which a sentence has meaning is an integral part of interpreting the meaning of the sentence. Take, for example, the sentence, "I am in the red." If the frame or simply the context of the sentence is motor racing, the sentence is likely about a tachometer reading, indicating that too much is being demanded of an engine. If, however, the frame is business performance, the sentence is likely about a business doing badly. Unless a computer recognizes the frame of a passage being translated, it will be unable to distinguish between such alternative meanings of the sentence. Lakoff (2006) provides an introduction to this analysis.
12. Thomas Kuhn (1996) posits a similar stickiness in the shift from one scientific paradigm to another. Rather than the advancement of science being a continuous accumulation of concept and evidence, Kuhn sees that advancement as jumping from one paradigm to another, the acceptance of a new paradigm being something of a leap of faith to a new way of looking at things that eventually demonstrates itself to be productive. Such a shift, his analysis implies, has social (status) implications among scientists, and these implications—as well as scientific evidence—influence the shifts.
13. The reform government in Argentina in the 1990s shared such an attitude.
14. Raúl Prebisch (1950) was one of the first to formalize this perspective.

References

Acemoglu, Daron, and James Robinson. 2012. *Why Nations Fail: The Origins of Power, Prosperity, and Poverty*. New York: Crown.

ADN Mundo. 2007. "China responde a las restricciones argentinas con una amenaza." August 27. http://www.adnmundo.com/contenidos/economia/argentina_china_conflictos_comerciales_ce_270807.html.

Boeninger, Iris. 2010. "Industria alimentaria: Oportunidades en mercados latinoamericanos—Argentina." Embajada de Chile, Buenos Aires.

Delletore, Raúl. 2011. "Trabajo argentino hasta en el último clavo." *Página 12*, November 30. http://www.pagina12.com.ar/diario/economia/2-182361-2011-11-30.html.

García Pérez, Alan. 2011. *Contra el temor económico: Creer en el Perú* [Against Economic Fear: Believing in Peru]. Lima: Planeta.

Global Trade Alert. 2010a. "Argentina: Legislation for Locally-Produced Motorcycles and Motorcycles-Parts Subsidies Program." Global Trade Alert, London. http://www.globaltradealert.org/measure/argentina-legislation-locally-produced-motorcycles-and-motorcycles-parts-subsidies-program.

———. 2010b. "Argentina Limits Entry Points for Certain Goods." Global Trade Alert, London. http://www.globaltradealert.org/measure/argentina-limits-entry-points-certain-goods.

———. 2011a. "Argentina Announces Import-Export-Balance Policy in the Automotive Industry." Global Trade Alert, London. http://www.globaltradealert.org/measure/argentina-announces-import-export-balance-policy-automotive-industry.

———. 2011b. "Argentina Extents Its Import-Export-Balance Policy to the Pharmaceutical Industry." Global Trade Alert, London. http://www.globaltradealert.org/measure/argentina-extends-its-import-export-balance-policy-pharmaceutical-industry.

———. 2011c. "Argentina: Import-Export '1 to 1' Policy Extended to Refrigerators, Washing Machines, Cookers, and Toys." Global Trade Alert, London. http://www.globaltradealert.org/measure/argentina-import-export-%E2%80%9C1-1%E2%80%9D-policy-extended-refrigerators-washing-machines-cookers-and-toy.

Hufbauer, Gary Clyde, and Sean Lowry. 2012. "U.S. Tire Tariffs: Saving Few Jobs at High Cost." Policy Brief 12-9, Peterson Institute for International Economics, Washington, DC.

Infocampo. 2012. "Pidien a la industria de la maquinaria que reduzca el déficit commercial." March 22. http://infocampo.com.ar/nota/campo/30852/pidien-a-la-industria-de-la-maquinaria-que-reduzca-el-deficit-comercial.

iProfessional.com. 2007. "Nueva batería de medidas para contener el avance chino." August 17. http://www.iprofesional.com/notas/51699-Nueva-batera-de-medidas-para-contener-el-avance-chino.

Kuhn, Thomas S. 1996. *The Structure of Scientific Revolutions*. 3rd ed. Chicago, IL: University of Chicago Press.

Lakoff, George. 2006. "Simple Framing: An Introduction to Framing and Its Uses in Politics." Rockridge Institute, Berkeley, CA. http://integral-options.blogspot.com/2009/04/simple-framing-by-george-lakoff.html.

McCarthy, Nigel. 2000. "Alf Rattigan and the Journalists: Advocacy Journalism and Agenda Setting in the Australian Tariff Debate, 1963–1971." *Australian Journalism Review* 22 (2): 88–102.

MEF (Ministry of Economy and Finance). 2005. *Tariff Policy Guidelines*. Ministry Resolution 005-2006-EF/15. Lima: MEF. http://www.mef.gob.pe/contenidos/pol_econ/econ_internac/resoluciones/rm005-2006ef15.pdf.

Ministry of Industry. 2011a. "Garbarino presentó un proyecto de inversión para fabricar tablets en Tierra del Fuego." Press Release, January 20. http://www.industria.gob.ar/garbarino-presento-un-proyecto-de-inversion-para-fabricar-tablets-en-tierra-del-fuego/.

———. 2011b. "Giorgi: Este gobierno cree y aplica administración del comercio." Press Release, February 25. http://www.industria.gob.ar/giorgi-este-gobierno-cree-y-aplica-administracion-del-comercio/.

———. 2011c. "La defense del mercado interno es un pilar fundamental para el crecimiento de la economía." Press Release, February 22. http://www.sub-industria.gob.ar/blog/2011/02/22/%e2%80%9cla-defensa-del-mercado-interno-es-un-pilar-fundamental-para-el-crecimiento-de-la-economia%e2%80%9d/.

———. 2012. "Giorgi: "el que más rápido integre piezas nacionales es el que más va a ganar." Press Release, March 22. http://www.industria.gob.ar/giorgi-el-que-mas-rapido-integre-piezas-nacionales-es-el-que-mas-va-a-ganar/.

Nogués, Julio J., and Elías A. Baracat. 2006. "Political Economy of Antidumping and Safeguards in Argentina." In *Safeguards and Antidumping in Latin American Trade Liberalization: Fighting Fire with Fire*, edited by J. Michael Finger and Julio J. Nogués, 45–78. New York: Palgrave Macmillan.

North, Douglass C. 1990. *Institutions, Institutional Change, and Economic Performance*. Cambridge, U.K.: Cambridge University Press.

Prebisch, Raúl. 1950. "The Economic Development of Latin America and Its Principal Problems." United Nations, New York.

Río Negro. 2012. "Récord de ventas de motovehículos durante el año pasado, con 716.207 unidades." May 27. http://www.rionegro.com.ar/diario/record-de-ventas-de-motovehiculos-durante-el-ano-pasado-con-716-207-unidades-880836-10944-notas_eco.aspx.

Secretariat of Public Communication. 2011. "Giorgi confirmo respaldo al sector textil y pidió más inversions." Press Release, June 22. http://www.prensa.argentina.ar/2011/06/22/20917-giorgi-confirmo-respaldo-al-sector-textil-y-pidio-mas-inversiones.php.

Webb, Richard, Josefina Camminati, and Raúl León Thorne. 2006. "Antidumping Mechanisms and Safeguards in Peru." In *Safeguards and Antidumping in Latin American Trade Liberalization: Fighting Fire with Fire*, edited by J. Michael Finger and Julio J. Nogués, 247–77. New York: Palgrave Macmillan.

Williamson, Oliver E. 2000. "The New Institutional Economics: Taking Stock." *Journal of Economic Literature* 38 (3): 595–613.

CHAPTER 5

Conclusions

Introduction

In this concluding chapter, we offer suggestions as to how the international community can support continuing trade policy reform. Interspersed with these suggestions is an evaluation of the capacities of institutional economics and the more limited political economy of trade reform as analytical frameworks for understanding the dynamics of trade reform and for shaping suggestions on how the international community might support further reform.

The general thesis of these conclusions is that liberalization is at its core a national decision. Its dynamic path is determined by a constellation of domestic political and economic forces, a few of which are influenced by international negotiations and agreements. The Peru case demonstrates how a government that is convinced that an open trade policy will serve the interests of its citizens can use international negotiations and the standards incorporated in international agreements to explain the case for liberalization to its citizens and to build support for such policies. The Argentina case demonstrates that international commitments per se will not prevent a government from adopting the opposite strategy. Likewise, international cooperation has been useful when it has recognized domestic sovereignty over economic regulation but useless when approached as a matter of international regulation of national actions.

Because the discussion's general thesis is that liberalization is a national decision, the thrust of our recommendations to the international community is that its attention be focused less on support for international negotiations and more on the domestic processes through which trade policy is made and the interests that shape such processes. This approach involves a double shift of emphasis (a) from international to domestic and (b) from result to process. The success of a liberalization program depends on how well it establishes in the national culture transparent and participatory processes that accurately weigh the impact of trade policy on all affected parties.

We want to call attention to the entire constellation of forces that influence trade policy in an effort to balance the romance of international negotiations against the realities of the domestic politics of trade. Our case studies indicate that much is to be learned from looking at national strategies for maintaining openness and, from that perspective, debating the ways by which international cooperation might support reform leaders. The opposite course has been more popular. But the realities we have contrasted as well as the lack of success of the World Trade Organization (WTO) Doha Round suggest that, at least for the moment, multilateral negotiations have exhausted their usefulness. There are other ways to frame the making of trade policy.

The remainder of this chapter elaborates those points.

Commitment Is Nothing If It Does Not Create Importer Rights in National Law and Regulation

We documented in chapter 1 that the school of thought often labeled *the political economy of trade reform* approaches policy as the outcome of a process of international negotiation. These negotiations simultaneously determine the trade policies of all countries—at least all the countries modeled. This approach does not accurately describe the liberalization experiences of Peru and Argentina, nor those of most of Latin America. Even so, information on new restrictions serves most often as a prelude to a call for renewed attention on multilateral negotiations (see, for example, Lamy 2012) rather than for attention on how to support governments in their management of domestic pressures for protection. The reason may be that the reigning political economy of trade reform has little to offer on such management—as we will discuss later.

As to the validity of the commitments model, it is clear from what we have learned that binding its tariffs and taking on the obligations of the Uruguay Round agreements as a member of the WTO—and accepting those of Mercado Común del Sur, or the Common Market of the South (MERCOSUR) as well—did not effectively lock in trade reforms in Argentina. WTO rules and WTO processes have not prevented Argentina's return its old system: an import substitution strategy and a system of trade policy governance that does not incorporate the procedural values of the WTO system.

As to interpreting *commitment* in a broader context, we reported in *Safeguards and Antidumping in Latin American Trade Liberalization: Fighting Fire with Fire* (Finger and Nogués 2006) that creating safeguard and antidumping mechanisms was an important part of the bargain to gain industry acceptance of reform. Acceptance by industry of the idea that it could cope with international competition was paired with the promise that it would be protected from abnormal or unfair competition. This bargain was political and was expressed in speeches and other public statements, often with reference to the rules and mechanisms of the General Agreement on Tariffs and Trade (GATT) and the WTO as the standard for distinguishing what industry would and would not be expected to accept.

Moreover, the GATT/WTO system that allowed only certain forms of trade restrictions—once transferred into domestic legislation—provided the basis in *domestic politics* for governments to eliminate the previously accumulated ad hoc mechanisms of trade control and to set up new procedures within agencies with economywide responsibilities and accountabilities.

Extending this analysis, meaningful commitment is about institutionalization in *national practice* of the right to import. In the modern value-chain economy, a guarantee in *national law* of enterprises' access to imports is more commercially relevant than the rights of exporters' governments to market access under WTO law.

A useful way to establish this point is with reference to tariff bindings versus the tariff rates that are specified in national law. The status of a tariff rate in national law can provide an immediate fix for an importer who is overcharged. Enforcing a bound rate through the WTO Dispute Settlement Understanding would be a lengthy and cumbersome process. First, the importing company would have to convince the exporting company to take the matter to its government. If the exporting country's government chose to take the matter to the WTO under the WTO Dispute Settlement Understanding, there would first be 60 days of consultations with the importing country's government. After that, the issue would come to the panel process and possibly the Appellate Body. Producing a panel report would consume six to nine months, and the Dispute Settlement Understanding allows 60 days for the WTO membership to adopt or reject the panel's report. If the losing party appeals to the Appellate Body, more time will elapse.[1] Even if the ruling favored the exporting country, in many importing countries that ruling would not create an obligation in national law to change the rate charged.

Thus, commitment, to have commercial value, is more than accepting an international legal obligation; it is translating that commitment into specific rights of private parties in the domestic economy, enforced through the domestic legal system. If officials in strict rule-of-law countries had imposed many of the restrictions imposed in Argentina, they would have been stopped immediately under domestic law.

Part of a property rights interpretation of trade remedies is that they express the rights of domestic industries to protection from foreign competition. In a rule-of-law situation—which implies a positive list approach to actions that the government can take—trade remedies also express limits on this right. Restrictions may be imposed only in specified situations and when the existence of those conditions has been established through specified procedures. These limits thus constitute the rights of importers to access to foreign goods.

Although the Argentine government, as a GATT/WTO member, has accepted an obligation to use only approved methods of trade control, no parallel limitation has evolved that is effective in Argentine law. There have been no effective legal challenges within Argentina against the new forms of restrictions. To be sure, Argentina has a liberal constitution, its treatment of trade (article 14) inspired by the rights and obligations of the U.S. constitution regarding freedom to trade. Even so, actual practice indicates that in Argentina the ad hoc actions by the government to restrict trade can be contested only at the level of general politics—for example, opposition to the government in the next election.

In Peru, all of the new restrictions that Global Trade Alert has identified have been managed through the trade remedies processes of the National Institute for the Defense of Competition and the Protection of Intellectual Property. Viewed from an institutional perspective, these mechanisms have passed through the initial steps of becoming institutions—of being accepted by interested parties as the appropriate way to deal with such matters.

Maintain the Momentum of Liberalization

The Argentine experience of the past decade is perhaps an exception. In all but a few countries, retreating from earlier reforms has been minimal. A recent World Bank review of the import strategies of developing countries found less risk that these governments will shift back to an import substitution strategy than that they will be overwhelmed by day-to-day pressures that current economic conditions have brought forward (Haddad and Shepherd 2011).

Focus on National Process

In this section, we address first how the international community might support a government that is attempting to maintain an open trade policy in the face of considerable pressure from domestic industries for protection. In this situation, we suggest that the conversation between the supporting international organization and countries begin with the following approach: "I accept that you are serious about maintaining your policy of openness—and that you are at present under considerable pressure from some industries for protection. I suggest we talk about how you might manage such pressures and what other countries' experiences have been." In this situation, the challenge of maintaining an open trade policy is to have in place systematic procedures for managing such pressures.[2]

This approach should help governments keep protection seekers in the system while generating insufficient protection to undo the dynamic of a liberal system. The approach does not necessarily entail an exact alignment of decisions on petitions for protection with the immediate logic of economic theory. "One step backward to preserve two steps forward" crudely describes the logic of such institutions.

The flexibilities or trade remedies or trade defense mechanisms provided for in GATT 1994 and the Uruguay Round agreements provide a good template for such mechanisms. The GATT/WTO procedural rules for trade remedies provide for (a) the recognition of and participation by interested parties, (b) open procedures according to previously announced criteria, and (c) publication of the decisions and the reasons for decisions—in fact and in law. They also prescribe time limits or periodic review of the usefulness of keeping a restriction in place. In short, the GATT/WTO rules provide for accountable, contestable processes that are based on criteria that have operational meaning, in which all stakeholders have an opportunity to participate.

Country officials might reply that their restrictions are (arguably) allowed by another WTO agreement, perhaps the agreement on sanitary and phytosanitary measures. This response might lead to a conversation on two points:

- The GATT/WTO rules are in large part compromises between interests that want protection and those that do not; they are not necessarily a guide for good policy.
- Some of the GATT/WTO agreements that allow trade restrictions prescribe procedures for taking into account the views of interested parties, whereas others, such as those for applying sanitary or phytosanitary measure, do not.

Particularly because we have evidence that restrictions on food imports have a strong negative effect on lower-income people,[3] governments might consider a more complete evaluation of the impact on interested parties than the WTO rules demand here. The good sense of the GATT/WTO procedural guidelines can be applied even where the GATT/WTO does not demand such.

Finally, we emphasize that the institutions that will evolve—though they will imbed similar economics—might be quite different politically and socially. Starting points and the general contexts of government procedures can be different.[4] In Australia, trade policy is strongly influenced by the economywide impact analysis provided by the Australian Productivity Commission. In the United States, a more legalistic, adversarial process typified by the trade remedies has evolved. This process is influenced more by the general reform of administrative procedures compelled by the U.S. Administrative Procedure Act and Freedom of Information Act than by the immediate demands of trade policy (Finger 2012). In the European Union (EU), the application of the community interest principle and of the lesser duty rule has provided a way of taking user interests into account. In addition, the EU decision process requires a vote by representatives of member states, and member states with minimal production of the product in question often defend the interests of users.[5] In Peru, as elaborated in chapter 2, the management of pressures for protection is evolving around the increasing confidence that is emerging in political as well as business circles in the National Institute for the Defense of Competition and the Protection of Intellectual Property.

An important part of Latin American reforms has been to replace the multitude of ad hoc procedures for managing pressures for protection with GATT/WTO-sanctioned procedures that provide transparent evaluation from the perspective of all interested parties. Not all GATT/WTO allowances for trade restrictions impose such procedural requirements—for example, sanitary and phytosanitary measures. The challenge now is to be more GATT/WTO than GATT/WTO—for national governments to impose such requirements even where GATT/WTO does not demand them, applying such procedures because they make economic and governance sense, rather than because the GATT/WTO mandates them.

Advocating such an approach can be dynamic politics. According to Australian Prime Minister Kevin Rudd (2008), "Evidence-based policy making is at the heart of being a reformist government."[6]

Notes

1. The European Union and 10 Latin American countries signed an agreement on November 8, 2012, that settled what the WTO (2012) described as "the longest-running series of disputes in the history of the multilateral trading system." The "bananas dispute" began in 1992, as a case under the GATT dispute settlement process.
2. A referee's comment on an earlier application of institutional economics to trade policy suggests an attitude that would be particularly unhelpful: "The paper could also be improved by acknowledging that there are sometimes good economic rationales for certain types of trade protection but that it is their abuse by policymakers (again acting in their own self-interest) that is the problem." Based on this interpretation, the conversation would begin by telling country officials that they were abusing good economic rationales for their own benefit. It would likely end there as well.
3. Anderson, Cockburn, and Martin (2010) provide a summary of and references to extensive research on the impact of trade protection on poverty. Even in the rural sector, many lower-income people, including farmers, purchase rather than produce much of their food. The impact of protection on them as consumers often outweighs its impact on them as producers.
4. Levy (2011, 60) takes up this point, voiced from the inverse perspective that "a country's economic, social, and political institutions cannot be re-engineered from scratch."
5. De Bièvre and Eckhardt (2010). The general evolution of administrative law in the EU is taken up by Kelemen (2011). Kelemen argues that the EU process is becoming more adversarial, but it is quite different from the way things are done in the United States.
6. The statement is quoted in Banks (2010, 248).

References

Anderson, Kym, John Cockburn, and Will Martin. 2010. "Introduction and Summary." In *Agricultural Price Distortions, Inequality, and Poverty*, edited by Kym Anderson, John Cockburn, and Will Martin, 3–45. Washington, DC: World Bank. http://siteresources.worldbank.org/INTTRADERESEARCH/Resources/544824-1272467194981/Ag_Price_Distortions_Inequality_Poverty_0310.pdf.

Banks, Gary. 2010. *An Economy-Wide View: Speeches on Structural Reform*. Melbourne, Australia: Productivity Commission.

De Bièvre, Dirk, and Jappe Eckhardt. 2010. "The Political Economy of EU Anti-Dumping Reform." ECIPE Working Paper 3/2010, European Centre for International Political Economy, Brussels.

Finger, J. Michael. 2012. "Flexibilities, Rules, and Trade Remedies in the GATT/WTO System." In *The Oxford Handbook on the World Trade Organization*, edited by Amrita Narlikar, Martin Daunton, and Robert M. Stern, 418–40. Oxford, U.K.: Oxford University Press.

Finger, J. Michael, and Julio J. Nogués, eds. 2006. *Safeguards and Antidumping in Latin American Trade Liberalization: Fighting Fire with Fire*. New York: Palgrave Macmillan.

Haddad, Mona, and Ben Shepherd, eds. 2011. *Managing Openness: Trade and Outward-Oriented Growth after the Crisis*. Washington, DC: World Bank.

Kelemen, R. Daniel. 2011. *Eurolegalism: The Transformation of Law and Regulation in the European Union*. Cambridge, MA: Harvard University Press.

Lamy, Pascal. 2012. "Rise in Trade Restrictions Now 'Alarming.'" Remarks at an informal meeting of heads of delegations to the World Trade Organization, Geneva, June 7. http://www.wto.org/english/news_e/sppl_e/sppl234_e.htm.

Levy, Brian. 2011. "The Politics of Development," *Development Outreach* 13 (1): 59–63.

Rudd, Kevin Michael. 2008. "Address to Heads of Agencies and Members of the Senior Executive Service." Great Hall, Parliament House, Canberra, April 30.

WTO (World Trade Organization). 2012. "Historic Signing Ends 20 Years of EU–Latin American Banana Disputes." Press Release, November 8. http://www.wto.org/english/news_e/news12_e/disp_08nov12_e.htm.

Environmental Benefits Statement

The World Bank is committed to reducing its environmental footprint. In support of this commitment, the Office of the Publisher leverages electronic publishing options and print-on-demand technology, which is located in regional hubs worldwide. Together, these initiatives enable print runs to be lowered and shipping distances decreased, resulting in reduced paper consumption, chemical use, greenhouse gas emissions, and waste.

The Office of the Publisher follows the recommended standards for paper use set by the Green Press Initiative. Whenever possible, books are printed on 50% to 100% postconsumer recycled paper, and at least 50% of the fiber in our book paper is either unbleached or bleached using Totally Chlorine Free (TCF), Processed Chlorine Free (PCF), or Enhanced Elemental Chlorine Free (EECF) processes.

More information about the Bank's environmental philosophy can be found at http://crinfo.worldbank.org/crinfo/environmental_responsibility/index.html.

green press INITIATIVE

www.ingramcontent.com/pod-product-compliance
Lightning Source LLC
Chambersburg PA
CBHW080614270326
41928CB00016B/3057
9780821399866